The Novels of John Gardner

The
Novels of
John Gardner

Making Life Art as a Moral Process

LEONARD BUTTS

LOUISIANA STATE UNIVERSITY PRESS
Baton Rouge and London

Designer: Sylvia Loftin
Typeface: English Times
Typesetter: Focus Graphics
Printer: Thomson-Shore, Inc.
Binder: John H. Dekker & Sons, Inc.

10   9   8   7   6   5   4   3   2   1

Library of Congress Cataloging-in-Publication Data
Butts, Leonard C.
The novels of John Gardner : making life art as a moral process /
Leonard Butts
    p. cm.
Bibliography: p.
Includes index.
ISBN 0-8071-1392-1
1. Gardner, John, 1933-   —Criticism and interpretation.
1. Title.
PS3557.A712Z58 1988
813'.54—dc19   87-25361
                                                               CIP

To Kathy and Lauren

That like the crocus budding through the snow—
That like a swimmer rising from the deep—
That like a burning secret which doth go
Even from the bosom that would hoard and keep;
Emerge thou mayst from the last whelming sea,
And prove that death but routs life into victory.

—HERMAN MELVILLE

Contents

Preface

When I began reading John Gardner's fiction several years ago, only four critical articles on his work had been published. Despite Gardner's success as a novelist, his identification with metafiction, and the numerous interviews he granted, critical attention to his work was not aroused to any great extent until the publication of *On Moral Fiction* in 1978. With what appeared to be such a didactic touchstone for his fiction, critics were eager to join in the fray produced by Gardner's attack on the "immoral" practices of fellow novelists. At a time when the Moral Majority movement made headlines nearly every day, Gardner's "moral treatise" on literature was an easy target not only for critics but also for reviewers, fellow fiction writers, politicians, and religious leaders.

Gardner was certainly one of the greatest publicists for his own work. This is evidenced not only by the debates he had with John Barth and William Gass over moral fiction and by appearances on radio and television, but also by the large number of interviews he granted to scholars, critics, journalists, and interested readers. He seldom turned down an invitation to speak about his work and about literature in general. But the problem with what soon became an avalanche of attention to *On Moral Fiction* was the degree to which each commentator projected his or her own feelings about morality and morals onto the subject of literature. As Joe David Bellamy's *Moral Fiction* anthology makes clear, even the most erudite and far-ranging of spokespersons for the contemporary literary scene — John Updike, Joyce Carol Oates, John Barth — responded not to Gardner's argument in *On Moral Fiction* but with their own feelings about what morality in literature is or should be.[1] In this light, it is difficult to assess the validity of what Bellamy hoped would be informed and intelligent responses to *On Moral Fiction*, yet Bellamy's collection does serve to point out how often critics and writers have reacted to the phrase *moral fiction* rather than to John Gardner's use of the term as it applies to literature. It is also apparent that use of the word *moral* sends many who have read Gardner's book into wild, emotional condemnations or praises, but often for the wrong

1. Joe David Bellamy (ed.), *Moral Fiction: An Anthology* (Canton, N.Y., 1980).

reasons. As with other well-worn terms—*romanticism, classicism, realism*—pejorative applications of the word *moral* have supplanted artistic, critical, and philosophical usage to such an extent that the word is crippled when pressed into a literary context. Despite the glee or grumbling of those who see Gardner's book as propaganda for fundamentalist religious beliefs or conservative political or literary stances, Gardner's theory of moral fiction has little to do with God or country or didactic fiction. Those who condemn or praise *On Moral Fiction* for these reasons have not understood Gardner's methods or purpose as a critic and as a novelist.

John Gardner's use of the word *moral* to define fiction containing some essence of universal truth can be grasped, however, through a statement that appears more than once in *On Moral Fiction*: "Art, in sworn opposition to chaos, discovers *by its process* what it can say."[2] If we keep in mind that the discovery of truth, assuming it exists, is reached in the *process* of creating, then much of the criticism leveled at Gardner for supposedly imposing an "artificial" order upon works of fiction can be dismissed. To suggest that a novel must have a "happy ending" or "present a moral" to be a work of "moral fiction" is to misinterpret Gardner's use of the phrase. In the same sense, to imply that because in one of Gardner's works the protagonist dies, in another is murdered, and in still another kills and eats a dog Gardner's fiction violates his own "moral principles" is also a misreading. Morality or truth, Gardner maintains (and for him the terms are inseparable), is not discovered in a novel's final lines, nor is it revealed entirely in any one character's actions. Morality or truth is discovered in the *process* of creating and in the *process* of reading a piece of fiction. It is the sum of a novel's or story's effect, what Aristotle calls its "exegesis," that determines its moral qualities.

As an artist, Gardner uses his imagination to test values and to get at what remnants of truth remain in a chaotic world. Art works, he argues, through an evolutionary process that ends in intense ordering. In this analogy, the imagination acts as a form of natural selection through which all experience is filtered and ordered. It is with the imagination that values are tested and truth, inherent morality, discovered. Only those values strong enough to withstand this testing survive and are passed on to the reader. If this process is "true," the art created from it will "naturally" instruct, raise human consciousness, and

2. John Gardner, *On Moral Fiction* (New York, 1978), 14.

offer a sense of wholeness or unity. Gardner's theory of fiction is based on the belief that the poet's imagination allows contact with "something far more deeply interfused," that within oneself exists an intuitive or implied mode for individual and social action. When the power of an artist's imagination is misdirected outward or fails altogether—if an artist is no longer able to look within himself and rediscover Dante's "liberating feeling" or Faulkner's "eternal verities," if he is no longer able to distinguish between intellectual game playing and truth—then he will not survive as an artist of lasting stature, even though his immediate influence on an audience and on other artists may be very great.

The process of creating to which Gardner refers is never directly revealed in a work of fiction, of course, although it may be discovered to some extent through the study of manuscripts and revisions of the work. Gardner allows us indirect access to this process in his fiction by portraying each character, on some level, as a kind of artist. In each of Gardner's novels we discover a protagonist in the midst of a physical and/or spiritual crisis, like Dante facing the dark wood. Attempting to wrest himself from such a situation, the individual asks whether solutions exist, if so what they are, and whether they will work. He also often encounters impasses or is misdirected by flaws in his own character or personality. But, as Gardner emphasizes, art is *not* merely a mirror held up to reality, and eventually the protagonist discovers some meaning, some order, some truth in his life. By "quietly looking and listening," as Gardner phrases it, the protagonist realizes through contact with the world and deep introspection certain values that eventually allow him to move toward a higher level of perception, an understanding closely akin to the aesthetically satisfying vision of an artist.

This search-and-discovery experience of the fictional protagonist in Gardner's novels parallels the process an artist undergoes in creating a work of art. The purpose of Gardner's own "moral fiction" is to discover what meaning life holds for us all, and not, as those who accuse him of writing didactically believe, to impose an external scheme of behavior upon everyone. In putting commonly held beliefs and values to the test, Gardner's fiction reveals amid crisis, chaos, and death not a simple rosy panacea of optimistic outcome but a process or method whereby those truths worth holding onto and passing on to future generations may be discovered. If we view each of Gardner's protagonists as an artist and his life as a work of art, we can more clearly understand what Gardner intends in his use of the phrase "moral fiction."

Although other critics and scholars have attempted to explicate *On Moral Fiction* through analysis of Gardner's philosophical argument (an argument that is essentially untenable because of its basis in feeling rather than in logic), Gardner's fiction, I believe, is the only acceptable "proof" for his beliefs, and his novels are the best illustrations of his methods and purpose. Each of the "moral artists" in *The Resurrection, Nickel Mountain, The Wreckage of Agathon, Grendel, The Sunlight Dialogues, October Light, Freddy's Book, Mickelsson's Ghosts, Stillness*, and *Shadows* is in search of some order, some insight to give life meaning, and at the same time each may be viewed as an artist journeying toward what he hopes will be a wholeness of vision, creating a work of lasting value, "making life art."

My intention is to analyze and to reflect upon the "evolutionary" way in which the protagonist of each novel moves toward a unifying vision or fails to break out of a limited vision of the world and his life. Through such an approach, I believe, we can see how each novel describes the arduous process of creating a work of art of lasting value. Because Gardner's focus on this process is so intense, he returns again and again to similar characters in slightly differing situations.

Although I began by organizing the study according to the chronology of the novels' composition (all of Gardner's books, fiction and nonfiction, were written in a different sequence than that in which they were published), I quite coincidentally discovered that the eight novels Gardner saw through publication can be paired according to striking similarities in characters, themes, and settings. James Chandler, the philosopher in *The Resurrection*, Gardner's first published novel, appears to be a younger version of Peter Mickelsson, the philosopher in *Mickelsson's Ghosts*, the novel published just before Gardner's death. Both novels deal more directly with philosophical and critical ideas than any of Gardner's nonacademic novels, with the exception of *The Sunlight Dialogues*. *Nickel Mountain* and *October Light* are united in the importance of their rural, pastoral settings. At the center of these least academic of Gardner's novels are nonintellectual protagonists, Henry Soames and James Page, who are attached to the land and the traditional values it embodies. Different still are the abrasive and anarchistic personalities of Taggert Hodge and Agathon in *The Sunlight Dialogues* and *The Wreckage of Agathon*. As enormously influential yet failed moral artists, they unite these two novels by their seerlike qualities and their roles as teachers of the moral artists Fred Clumly and Peeker. Perhaps the most intriguing pairing of novels arises from the monster-as-artist theme of *Grendel* and *Freddy's Book*. Gardner's portrait of the nihilistic vision of Jean-Paul Sartre in the monster Grendel is transformed into Gardner's own moral vision in the giant Freddy Agaard. An additional coincidence that has allowed my organizational method to remain consistent throughout this study is the decision of novelist Nicholas Delbanco, Gardner's literary executor, and Gardner's editors at Knopf to publish posthumously only a pair of incomplete novels from among his remaining manuscripts, and I have added a chapter to evaluate them. Because of the doubling so often used by Gardner within his novels, pairing the novels appears to be a most convenient and critically interesting means of organizing them. Despite the tendency of such an organizational method toward leveling—that is, to make each novel seem neither more nor less important than another—I think it is a method worth chancing, especially within the limited approach I am using. Nevertheless, in the conclusion of the study, I have tried to compensate for this leveling effect by offering a brief summary of the relative strengths and weaknesses of the novels.

A close reading of each of Gardner's protagonists as artists also reveals much about Gardner's thematic concerns and the values he believes can survive the entropy that pervades our lives and the lives of his characters. Since I began my work on Gardner with an investigation of his use of nature as "moral center" in *October Light*, I have discovered that each of Gardner's protagonists, in his search for meaning, inevitably retreats, in true Romantic fashion, into the natural world for comfort, peace, and recovery. Yet each must overcome the Romantic fallacy inherent in such a limited vision and accept not just the pastoral comfort but also the evolutionary randomness of death and survival—the "brute existent" of nature—of which each of us is a microcosm, in order to discover more lasting values within the physical world and within oneself. If nature does not dominate setting, as in *Nickel Mountain* and *October Light*, it still very much influences the characters who have had a connection of some importance with it. Usually associated with an imagined or real past, the natural world for Gardner's protagonists becomes a symbol of unity and stability to which they may retreat to shut out, at least temporarily, the confusing, shifting values of modern society. Although Gardner uses the city/country dichotomy often, he does not sentimentalize or make melodramatic the darker side of nature. When nature reveals its chaotic, "swirling, black clouds" of death, Gardner's protagonists come

to sense a primal force directing them not to oblivion but to an awareness that death is also a part of life and cannot be denied its place in
the totality of existence. Nature, because it is at once chaotic and orderly, wild and tame, violent and peaceful, randomly creative and
strictly selective, reflects the human condition. Gardner uses nature as
what Herman Melville called his "Greenwich Standard," or moral center, for it contains a portion of the necessary truth from which each individual can learn to incorporate all aspects of his existence and personality into a unified whole.

Since the movement into nature is most often a retreat into isolation, into oneself, a catalyst is necessary to recover some sense of
worth in the world at large. Just as Dante, Gardner's example of a
moral artist in *On Moral Fiction*, has Beatrice and/or Vergil by which
to gauge his moral character and to find his way out of the dark wood,
so each of Gardner's protagonists, if he is to survive, needs someone
to offer support and guidance in times of doubt and despair. In *On
Moral Fiction*, Gardner says of Dante that the poet arrived at a model
of art's function after struggling through a grave spiritual crisis when
even faith in the existence of God offered no consolation. From the
depths of depression over the death of Beatrice, Dante began to search
through his life for some meaning. He recognized only his deep and
vivid feeling for Beatrice, a person whose perfection, in Dante's mind
at least, would never allow him to lie, whose innate goodness and intelligence, as Gardner says, made Dante uncomfortably conscious of
behavior unnatural to his inner self. Beatrice becomes Dante's direct
link with God and a standard by which he measures his actions and the
actions of others. Such intercessors, Gardner is quick to point out, are
common in great literature, from Chaucer's knight to Shakespeare's
Ophelia to many of the heroes and heroines of Henry James.[3]

Similar characters, whom we might call "saintly intercessors," are
symbols of the sacrificial nature and compassion of love in Gardner's
novels. Although their origin is with Dante's Beatrice, these characters
are not depicted in the manner of the perfect being of *La vita nuova*,
but they do inspire and stimulate their "artists" to seek the truth about
themselves. Estelle Parks in *October Light*, Esther Clumly in *The Sunlight Dialogues,* Callie Wells in *Nickel Mountain,* and Jessica Stark in
Mickelsson's Ghosts are the most obvious examples. In using such a
device in his novels, Gardner leaves himself open to charges of sexism,

3. *Ibid.*, 34.

but he does develop these women far beyond the allegorical or stereo-typical female goddesses of the courtly lover or macho hero. For the moral artist, the saintly intercessor represents an ideal audience that he cannot deceive or betray with rhetorical games or sentimental pandering. The saintly intercessor moves the protagonist toward his goal of wholeness because she embodies the compassion he must have to attain any kind of reintegration with society.

Gardner's argument that such love and compassion must somehow be infused into the moral artist's work is put forth directly in *On Moral Fiction.* Like the word *moral,* Gardner explains, " 'Love' is of course another of those embarrassing words, perhaps a word even more embarrassing than 'morality,' but it's a word no aesthetician ought carelessly to drop from his vocabulary. Misused as it may be by pornographers and the makers of greeting-cards, it has, nonetheless, a firm, hard-headed sense that names the single quality without which true art cannot exist."[4]

To emphasize the need for human contact in the struggle to survive, if only momentarily, the yawning abyss of death and despair, Gardner often uses a gathering or communion of friends and family as an additional catalyst for the release of human feelings and emotions needed by the protagonist to complete his journey toward an affirmation of life. The gatherings in Gardner's novels reveal the fragility of life, the necessity of maintaining contact with the world, and the "connected-ness" each individual requires, because in order to "see" more fully one must have love and compassion not only for another individual but for all of humanity in its various guises. Gatherings that result in epiphanies or breaks in impasses occur in all of the novels. For the moral artist, the gathering represents the necessity of audience, the so-cial responsibility embodied in great art. As Gardner has said, art's purpose is to instruct, and the best artists are those who can reconcile their own artistic integrity with their responsibility to society.

Just as Dante learns from Vergil and from the testimony and examples of the souls in the inferno of hell, so Gardner's artist/pro-tagonists learn from teachers and from examples of failure. Gardner's "minor artists" — those secondary (but sometimes scene-stealing) char-acters who are failures at "making life art" — aid the moral artist in achieving his unified vision. Although two of these characters — Tag-gert Hodge and Agathon — profess to be teachers, they teach best by

4. *Ibid.,* 83.

being living examples of what the moral artist should avoid in his behavior and philosophy. These often pathetic figures also include, among others, George Loomis in *Nickel Mountain*, John Horne in *The Resurrection*, and Grendel.

Although Gardner's protagonists obviously cannot achieve their reintegrations alone—a reiteration of Gardner's belief that the artist who creates only for himself or without necessary contact with the world is doomed to failure—they do seem to contain, as do all of us, the necessary means for expanding and thereby increasing their understanding of life and the world. Suggestions of such inherent strength are reproduced in Gardner's novels through the many appearances of ghosts and ominous strangers. Often the ominousness of these figures is a result of their embodiment of some darker self or life the protagonist refuses to acknowledge. The most obvious ominous strangers occur in dreams in *The Resurrection*, in storms in *Nickel Mountain* and *October Light*, and as actual ghosts in *Mickelsson's Ghosts*. By recognizing or coming to understand the ominous stranger, the protagonist sees the limitations of his own idealism or self-righteousness or single-mindedness. For the moral artist, the ominous stranger is usually a harbinger of important knowledge.

Although John Gardner "practiced what he preached" and tried his hand, usually with some success, in many genres, my primary intention in this study is to reveal Gardner's process of moral fiction by pursuing those elements common to each novel's, and each protagonist's, movement toward affirmation. Readers, however, may find it odd that, in a book dealing with Gardner's fiction, there is so little mention of his short stories and children's tales. All of Gardner's fiction supports my thesis concerning the novels, but the weakness of the short stories and tales is that they are so direct and obvious (one might argue didactic) in presenting successful and failed moral artists. This result, of course, is partly due to the genre. The fairy tale calls for a moral and is didactic by nature, and the limitations of the short story force Gardner to abbreviate or omit most of the process or working out of values that we see in the novels, so the successes and failures of the protagonists are often realized before the narratives begin. And unlike the novels, the stories of *The King's Indian* and *The Art of Living* contain many protagonists who are artists rather than artist-figures. Taking Gardner's obviousness as it is intended, David Cowart in *Arches and Light: The Fiction of John Gardner* and Gregory Morris in *A World of Order and Light: The Fiction of John Gardner* include in their evaluations of the short story collections quite successful readings of Gardner's artists as either failures or successes at "making life art," and I see no need to repeat their accurate analyses.[5]

Perhaps the most important reason for not making my study comprehensive is that with two books and four collections of essays on Gardner's work already in print (all of which have been published since 1982), I believe it is necessary to begin a more detailed critical evaluation than overviews of the canon or individual articles on the novels or stories will allow. Since Gardner thought of himself primarily as a novelist, as interviews and his two books on fiction writing reveal, it is only logical to devote lengthier and more specific studies to the novels. Such concentrated attention, I think, will lead to a wider recognition of Gardner's genius and a more precise definition of his place in American literature. I hope, therefore, I am taking an obvious and necessary first step.

5. David Cowart, *Arches and Light: The Fiction of John Gardner* (Carbondale, Ill., 1983), 76-110, 165-87; Gregory L. Morris, *A World of Order and Light: The Fiction of John Gardner* (Athens, Ga., 1984), 116-42, 184-205.

Acknowledgments

Portions of this book have appeared in different forms in *Critique, MSS, John Gardner: True Art, Moral Art, Thor's Hammer: Essays on John Gardner, Tennessee Philological Bulletin,* and *South Atlantic Review.* I wish to thank once again all of the scholars of John Gardner's work with whom I have discussed and corresponded about Gardner's novels, and in particular Robert A. Morace, Gregory L. Morris, David Cowart, and Jeff Henderson. I also owe a special thanks to Nicholas Delbanco, John Howell, and Liz Rosenberg, who never hesitated to take time from their own work to help with details about Gardner's life and to encourage my efforts.

Extracts from *On Moral Fiction* (copyright © 1978) by John Gardner are reprinted by permission of Basic Books, Inc.

Extracts from *The Resurrection* (copyright © 1974) and *The Wreckage of Agathon* (copyright © 1970), both by John Gardner, are reprinted by permission of Georges Borchardt, Inc.

Extracts from *On Becoming a Novelist* (copyright © 1983) by John Gardner are reprinted by permission of Harper & Row, Publishers, Inc.

Extracts from "A Phenomenology of *On Moral Fiction,*" by Charles Johnson, published in *Thor's Hammer: Essays on John Gardner,* edited by Jeff Henderson, published by the University of Central Arkansas Press (copyright © 1985), are reprinted by permission of Charles Johnson.

Extracts from the following works of John Gardner — *The Art of Fiction: Notes on Craft for Young Writers* (copyright © 1984); *The Art of Living and Other Stories* (copyright © 1981); *Freddy's Book* (copyright © 1980); *Grendel* (copyright © 1971); *The King's Indian: Stories and Tales* (copyright © 1974); *Mickelsson's Ghosts* (copyright © 1982); *Nickel Mountain* (copyright © 1973); *October Light* (copyright © 1976); *Stillness and Shadows* (copyright © 1986); and *The Sunlight Dialogues* (copyright © 1972) — are reprinted with the permission of Random House, Inc./Alfred A. Knopf, Inc.

An extract from "Sunday Morning" by Wallace Stevens, from *The Collected Poems of Wallace Stevens* (copyright © 1982), is reprinted by permission of Alfred A. Knopf, Inc.

The Novels of John Gardner

1

Philosophical Castles

The Resurrection
and *Mickelsson's Ghosts*

The ultimate moral value, the moral value I
really look for beyond anything else, is to be exactly truthful — seeing things clearly, the *process*
of art. — JOHN GARDNER

The Resurrection

More than any of his other novels, John Gardner's *The Resurrection*
has been neglected by critics. Those who have evaluated Gardner's first
published novel have described it as flat, not clearly organized, and
overly philosophical. One might expect such condemnations from reviewers, but given the highly philosophical nature of Gardner's fiction
and the prolificity of his career, it is curious that *The Resurrection* is
so casually dismissed by critics as well.[1] Written during the same time
period as the first draft of *On Moral Fiction, The Resurrection* is the
fictional counterpart of Gardner's philosophical treatise on contemporary writing and criticism. Parts of *On Moral Fiction* appear verbatim
in protagonist James Chandler's metaphysical meditations, and in the
characters, plot, setting, and point of view, we see precedents for all
of Gardner's novels that follow, especially his particular technique of
revealing through the protagonist's struggles with life how the artist

---

1. For negative reactions of reviewers, see Robert A. Morace, *John Gardner: An Annotated Secondary Bibliography* (New York, 1984), 69–71. As for critical reaction,
Cowart, *Arches and Light*, indirectly dismisses the novel, along with *Nickel Mountain* and *The Wreckage of Agathon*, by placing all three together in a single chapter
focusing only on their pastoral aspects. Morris, *A World of Order and Light*, gives
The Resurrection its own chapter but decides it is a failure because "Gardner does
more 'telling' than 'showing,' and his characters turn flat and sometimes just unlike-
able" (228). One of the earliest evaluations of Gardner's novels — Susan Strehle,
"John Gardner's Novels: Affirmation and the Alien," *Critique*, XVIII (1976), 86–96
— says "affirmation is forced" in both *The Resurrection* and *Nickel Mountain*.

creates his art. [2] One might even argue that *The Resurrection* succeeds where *On Moral Fiction* fails, for the novel reveals the advantages of art over philosophy. While one may conveniently overlook Gardner's unpublished dissertation novel, *The Old Men*, as juvenilia, *The Resurrection* deserves a higher place in the canon and should not be relegated so quickly to obscurity by critics.

As in nearly all of Gardner's novels, death is the moving force of *The Resurrection*. Even before we are allowed to see James Chandler's gravesite in the opening scene, we are confronted with the title of the novel and all of its implications. Conceived as a reply to Tolstoy's *Resurrection* (the didacticism of which Gardner disliked), Gardner's novel reveals, and the title itself suggests, the saving grace toward which all of his protagonists grope—the "aesthetic wholeness" of his artists and philosophers and the "holy intuitive vision" of his nonintellectuals. James Chandler, the protagonist of the novel, is, as Gardner quickly reveals, an idealist. Living in San Francisco, surrounded by the fellowship of his family, friends, and work, in a serene state of disassociation from the harsher conditions of life, Chandler is sequestered within an "ivory tower" of his own design, even to the extent that he views himself as a kind of modern-day hero: "His concern with metaphysics in the age of analysis made him a man born too late for his time, a harmless lunatic all of whose energy and skill went into a heroic battling, by the laws of an intricate and obsolete code, against whatever he could contrive in the way of dragons." [3] When Chandler is confronted not with an abstract conceptualization of death but with the inevitability of his own death from leukemia, his philosophical dragons are reduced to a very real foe he cannot defeat, and the fortress of life he has created crumbles. Upon receiving the news that he has an incurable disease, Chandler, with his wife and three children, decides to retreat across the country to his hometown of Batavia, New York. Chandler's mother still lives in Batavia, and he associates a certain stability and security with growing up in the small town.

Any return into time or investigation of the past is, for American writers especially, a return to a simpler existence, to the natural world.

2. John Howell, "The Wound and The Albatross: John Gardner's Apprenticeship," in Jeff Henderson (ed.), *Thor's Hammer: Essays on John Gardner* (Conway, Ark., 1985), 1–16; Morris, *A World of Order and Light*, 33.
3. John Gardner, *The Resurrection* (New York, 1974), 11. Because of numerous corrections which Gardner made, the preferred text is this Ballantine paperback edition rather than the New American Library hardcover edition (1966). Further references to the Ballantine edition will be made in the text.

For Gardner's main characters, such a retreat is the first hopeful act on a journey toward a possible reordering of their lives. For James Chandler, the return across country from west to east is a movement back into the past of small-town America and nineteenth-century Romantic values. Less symbolically, it is a retreat from the certainty of death toward the hope offered by his origins. When the threat of extinction becomes personal, Chandler turns to his past in search of some answer to the apparent chaos and meaninglessness of the modern world. This past, so often associated with an Edenic or pastoral existence, provides some initial relief to the protagonist, but even though Gardner's novels offer various retreats — small-town Batavia, remote mountain hamlets, medieval Europe, classical Greece — the past and the natural world with which it is associated never contain satisfactory solutions for his protagonists' dilemmas. The Romantic retreat to nature is too simple an answer in Gardner's scheme of things.

Initially, as is the case with most terminal patients, Chandler's inability to comprehend the immediacy of his own death results in denial and anger.[4] When his wife Marie insists that he go to the hospital for tests after they arrive in Batavia, Chandler explodes in a violent verbal attack: "It seemed to him that he hated her unspeakably and had always hated her. . . . She'd become what she was: a pointless disposition of teeming atoms, brute Nature spiritless and overwhelming as the sound of a siren outside a music hall" (22). Although Chandler is horrified by such feelings, he is unable to deal with them. He wishes only to escape, to avoid the concern of his family that reminds him of his deteriorating condition.

Chandler's search for meaning begins as he sets out to explore the town of his youth, hoping to discover in Batavia some signs of concrete or material order to reinforce his memories. When he first walks the streets of his hometown, however, he is dismayed at how the pastoral world he remembers has been urbanized: "There was not a trace of the comfortable old country town, nothing" (36). In spite of his liberal politics, which include a belief that civilization is evolving toward an ideal social and economic state, Chandler begins to feel a conflict over the change necessary for such progress. When he is alone with his mother, he mourns that "when she died it would be the death of an age, a way of seeing; the end of the great Romantic return to Nature"

---

4. Whether consciously or not, Gardner moves Chandler through what Elisabeth Kubler-Ross, *On Death and Dying* (New York, 1969), 34–121, calls the "five stages of dying" — denial, anger, bargaining, depression, acceptance.

(32). Although he has come to believe it right that time eventually erases differences, that "in time, almost inevitably—only the death of earth could stop it—there would be peace between races as well, and nations; and the beauty of what had happened here would be raised to the billionth power," his Spencerian view is no longer sufficient explanation when he is faced with the ultimate change—his own death. "It was good," he thinks of his once-comforting utopian vision, "but it was *not* all right" (36). He also is not able to see that the passing of an age, such as the "great Romantic return to nature," does not necessarily mean an end to the metaphysics or aesthetics of that age, for, as Gardner argues, "an emotional system remains valid as long as people continue to feel that it is valid."[5] When Chandler realizes that, despite its overtures to progress, the pastoral town of his youth has been subject to the same entropy that affects his life, he insists that certain absolutes must exist. " 'Something must be certain,' " he thinks aloud as he wanders around his hometown, already knowing that his search for the stability of his childhood is futile.

Chandler continues his search for some external means of reassurance by visiting the Staley sisters. In the appearances and states of mind of the three sisters (the three Fates?), he finds only grotesque reminders of the effects of aging, but in the Staley house Chandler does encounter a symbol of his Edenic memory. Aunt Emma Staley's painting, "The Old Mill," appears to be only another reminder of the relentless entropic forces of nature. Gradually, however, James Chandler understands that in order to accept his own death, he needs the all-encompassing vision of the painting's creator.

Seeing the painting again in the house where he spent hours at piano lessons as a child, Chandler at first dismisses the work as amateurish and "tortuously rendered": "He had to smile now to think that he had once been so easily impressed" (51). Yet the longer he looks at the painting, the more absorbed in it he becomes and the more clearly he sees it from an intuitive rather than from an intellectual perspective: "One could see that the young Emma Staley had painted with feeling. In the sky, dark, mountainous thunderheads; below, ancient cypresses huddled together, pitted rocks, churning white water, the crumbling remains of the mill. All was motion and decay: It seemed to rot before one's very eyes" (51). When Chandler lets down his intellectual guard, the painting comes alive, and "all at once, without warning, even as he

<hr>

5. Gardner, *On Moral Fiction,* 171.

stood inwardly laughing at the painting, the old mood rose in him again: He felt a sudden, surprising unrest, a vague ardent thirst for the past, for wilderness, for freedom, for heaven knew what—a paradoxical sense of intense dissatisfaction with himself and, at the same time, a kind of vaulting joy" (51–52). The haunting effect of the painting is the first suggestion in the novel that Chandler's retreat may have some value. Although Gardner undercuts Chandler's expectations with grim reminders that the pastoral world of his childhood has long since disappeared, Emma Staley's vision, as revealed in "The Old Mill," has survived. As Gardner has suggested in *On Moral Fiction*, the evolutionary randomness and intense ordering of the natural world are analogous to the workings of the moral artist's imagination in creating a work of art.[6] The art produced in such a process often is of great intrinsic value. Like Freddy Agaard in *Freddy's Book*, Aunt Emma lacks the technique to produce a great work of art, but the effect of her painting on Chandler, who is receptive to her vision, is proof that her intuitions concerning the function a work of art should have are correct. "The Old Mill" takes as its subject the death and decay Chandler wishes to avoid, yet Aunt Emma's acceptance and celebration of her subject affirm the kind of vision Chandler must develop in order to discover any meaning in his life or in his death.

Like nearly all of Gardner's protagonists who possess an idyllic view of the past and who retreat into a pastoral world to rediscover that past, Chandler must learn that one cannot ignore or avoid the "brute forces" of nature, including the darker side of human nature, that push each of us toward oblivion. Gardner embraces the calm of a pastoral world and is, to a certain extent, appreciative of the Romantic view of nature as a healing influence and as a means of stripping away the complexities of modern life, but he seeks constantly to remind us that such a pastoral world either no longer exists or perhaps never existed except in the vivid imaginations of poets.

Chandler's myopic view (he literally has poor eyesight) of the past is further undercut by memories of his father, which suggest that his childhood was not so stable or idyllic as he wishes to believe. Chandler's philosophical idealism may be a reaction to his father's "infuriatingly logical" approach to life, in which he "tended to ride roughshod over disagreement and to view all emotion, aside from intellectual

6. See Jeff Henderson, "The Avenues of Mundane Salvation: Time and Change in the Fiction of John Gardner," *American Literature*, LV (1983), 611–33, for a thorough discussion of Gardner's use of evolutionary theory in his fiction.

emotion, with some distaste, as a thing subnormal" (126). Although Chandler recognizes his father's basic flaw as having mistaken "the laws of his own nature for absolutes," he has never been able to deal with the selfishness of his father's suicide: "For a long time afterward James Chandler had been tortured by nightmares in which his father pursued him with a gun" (126). Chandler's notion that he is somehow responsible for his father's death (nearly all of Gardner's novels contain a character who, like Gardner himself, is haunted by a family member's death) only adds to the despair he already feels and contributes to the guilt he soon begins to experience over neglecting his family in favor of his own personal search for values. To avoid his father's flaw, Chandler has fled analytical philosophy and embraced metaphysics. Yet in continuing to use only philosophical techniques to "chase intuitions," Chandler restricts his experience of life as much as his father did. Chandler's need to intellectualize everything leads him to believe that discovering a philosophical solution to the dilemma of his impending death is more important than spending his final days enjoying his family and friends. Preceding and following his collapse on the sidewalk in front of the Staley house—a turning point in his search and in his attitude toward death—Chandler encounters two people whom Gardner labels "freaks of nature" because their adherence to rigid systems of belief, as in the case of Chandler's father, has severely limited their visions and isolated them from the community. Viola Staley, the great-niece of the Staley sisters, and John Horne, a grotesquely fat law librarian, inadvertently aid James Chandler on his journey to wholeness, and their lives appear to represent the flawed art of "minor artists" in *The Resurrection*.

It is significant that Viola Staley refers to Aunt Emma's painting as "The Ruined Mill," for her life is the antithesis of Chandler's in its reliance upon feeling rather than on reason and in its embrace of sentimental notions of death. She "was unfit for Nature—especially just now. Spring, for her, was intolerable. It had always been: She could remember huddling against it as a child, feeling violated by sights and sounds and smells—not only the stench and racket of a neighbor's gasoline lawn mower but even the sick-sweet scent of trees, the music of birds, the movement of clouds above pines" (73). " 'She's evil,' " Chandler's mother Rose declares of Viola. Like Simon Bale in *Nickel Mountain*, Viola does appear to have been born at odds with the world. In addition to her aversion to nature, she is obsessed with the idea that death holds the kind of freedom for which she longs: "In dreams she would sometimes see herself, even now, in a golden casket with a polished glass lid, and faceless nuns would surround her white, still corpse. It was very moving to her, and poetic" (74). More than half in love with easeful death, Viola clings to a melancholy Romantic vision. While Chandler exists in a web of ideas and ideals and cannot cope with the reality of death, Viola cannot cope with the reality of living and embraces a sentimental vision of death as an escape and a comfort. As these two people begin to move toward one another, the reader gradually begins to see the kind of vision Gardner embraces. Life and death, of course, are parts of a whole, and any kind of true aesthetic vision must embrace both. Viola's self-absorption also serves as warning that Chandler's decision to isolate himself from his family and friends can only lead to further misreadings of his place in the total scheme of things.

Viola's struggle against life is intensified when she is drawn into the Chandler family and finds herself caught between the roles of care-taker of the three ancient Staley sisters and "guardian" of Chandler's three young daughters. She relishes this new involvement and is hap-pier still when she is able to rush Chandler to the hospital after he col-lapses in front of the Staley house. Viola is, in effect, attracted to Chandler because he is dying, moving toward what she believes is a fi-nal and beautiful peace. In Viola's view, Chandler is a heroic Roman-tic figure because he is being cut down in the "prime of life": "The truth was, she was glad he had fallen to the sidewalk, bleeding, glad she had been there, glad to feel his cold blood on her dress. Like one watching a liner sink or watching a new motel burn down, Viola felt intensely alive, favored by the gods, and her secret awareness that she was glad made her cheeks and forehead burn with shame" (80-81). In Viola, Gardner creates the "minor artist" who strives for the sensa-tional and melodramatic in art (life). Interested only in vicarious thrills, such an artist, Gardner argues, never considers the repercus-sions her work may have among readers. Viola's feelings about life and death have isolated her from other "angles of vision" and have made her a disagreeable creature to those characters, such as Chand-ler's wife and mother, who possess a more affirmative outlook.

Yet Viola is more than a one-dimensional figure, for Gardner is al-ways careful to flesh out even his less-likable characters, and critics and reviewers who believe *The Resurrection* fails because it favors philosophical discourse over character development have not looked carefully at minor characters like Viola Staley. Despite her eccentric personality, Viola is able to love, and just as Simon Bale, the "evil" religious fanatic in *Nickel Mountain*, is moved by the love of a young child, Viola exults in the Chandler children's innocent friendship. Viola also fears rejection, even by people like Marie and Rose Chandler, whom she despises. As with so many of Gardner's doomed characters — his "minor artists" — Viola Staley is trapped by irrational feelings of jealousy, envy, despair, and above all guilt, and unlike Gardner's moral artists, she cannot see her way free of her entrapment. Her confession of love for James Chandler becomes a sad yet necessary sacrifice to move Chandler from his existence among vague ideas into an acceptance of reality.

In the pitiable character of John Horne, law librarian and amateur philosopher, Gardner parodies Chandler's philosophical approach to life. Like Viola Staley, Horne is overwhelmed by despair. In the hospital and apparently on the verge of death himself, Horne is frightened at the meaninglessness of the life he has lived and tries to reach some consolation by philosophizing. In his conversation with Chandler, Horne reveals the limited, deterministic vision he has embraced. He believes that he has "no function—whether by virtue of his character or by virtue of his social condition" (151): " 'You don't even *actively* change your life. You happen to see or you happen *not* to by virtue of a health or sickness deeper than consciousness' " (149). John Horne sees life in terms of absolutes, and for Horne " 'Art is atonement. . . . Good poets atone for the evil in their lives, evil poets atone for the evil in their very souls, which they cannot help but continue to affirm' " (149). As an artist, Horne would use art merely to satisfy some inner need or to vent frustration or guilt rather than to make connection with an audience. Gardner admits that "bibliotherapy" seems to work, and did work for him in dealing with his brother Gilbert's death, but true art, Gardner believes, should have a function beyond alleviating an artist's personal problems.[7]

Horne is crushed when Chandler points out the flaw in his argument: " 'You insist on finalities,' Chandler said, '—if not final salvation then final damnation, no mixture of judgments.' " (152). Both Viola Staley and John Horne seek "charity" from Chandler; acceptance by other human beings within a community, Gardner suggests, is one of the more powerful needs of every individual. Like Viola, Horne is isolated by his insistence upon the vision he has formulated, and he

---

7. Howell, "The Wound and the Albatross," 6.

cannot make his desire for acceptance known to Chandler. When Chandler rejects his philosophical posturing, Horne is able only to emit a pathetic nonverbal plea for blessing: "I need you, you don't need me. Nothing to do with the pitch of the mind, Mr. Chandler. Have mercy on me!" (181). For Horne, Chandler's departure is the final rejection, the loss of his last hope of salvation through human contact. Ironically, Chandler faces the same isolation as Viola and Horne. Viola and Horne are in search of acceptance and love, but their very natures repel people; Chandler needs acceptance and love, but he rejects people, family and strangers alike, who are drawn to him. Just as Viola represents the darker side of each of us that Chandler refuses to recognize in himself, so John Horne, like Chandler's father, represents through his insistence on reason the ultimate isolation for which Chandler seems destined.

Chandler ignores these examples of failure cast in his path by chance. Because he believes his external search for meaning is exhausted even before he collapses, he isolates himself still further from human contact by deciding to pursue an internal search for meaning. If he can complete his book, Chandler believes, and in doing so develop a metaphysical system that will offer lasting comfort and hope, he may gain a kind of immortality and at the same time make his life meaningful.

Although Chandler could finish his metaphysical treatise on aesthetics by following the same course of thinking as philosopher R. G. Collingwood—Gardner's model for Chandler—does in *Principles of Art* or as Gardner himself does in *On Moral Fiction,* Gardner has a slightly different point to make. In *On Moral Fiction*, Gardner argues that moral fiction evolves from a certain kind of creative process, but in his novels he wishes to dramatize this belief. As time runs short for Chandler, the leukemia and the drugs he takes to delay its progress begin to affect his thinking, and he becomes frustrated at his inability to reason. Yet through his dreams, Chandler begins to engage the imaginative process of art that will finally bring some order into his life. His dreams begin to take on the shape of conscious creations, "an imaginative work of selection and arrangement. . . . He had the conviction, as he dreamed, that he was creating an artistic masterpiece" (123). When he wakes, he finds his conviction ludicrous, yet "even as Chandler laughed, something came to him, or rather hovered in the periphery of his inner vision, so to speak, an idea that he could not quite catch hold of, but one that was right—that much he could feel— some insight that might be, at least for him, revolutionary" (123). Because Chandler cannot bring the idea to consciousness, he fails momentarily as a philosopher and as a moral artist, for Gardner shares Collingwood's belief that "the function of imagination is to raise what is 'preconscious' (for instance, mere feeling) to consciousness by giving it definite form."[8] Chandler does give symbolic form to the idea, however, for in his dream he encounters an "intruder"—the old woman with a mouthful of blood (39).

This intruder or "ominous stranger" occurs in all of Gardner's novels and often represents the knowledge needed by the artist/protagonist to achieve a higher level of perception. In *The Resurrection*, the intruder in Chandler's dream is a symbol of the death and decay inherent in life, and of Aunt Emma, whose artistic vision embraces the totality of existence. Although in devising a suitable defense for his study of metaphysics Chandler has come to believe "whereas in Nature human consciousness discovers and enlarges itself by learning to categorize and choose between brute sensations (or the emotional charge in brute sensations) and later to choose between passions, in Art a gifted consciousness simplifies, extends or reorders categorization and choice for the rest of us, speeding up the painfully slow process of evolution toward what, hopefully, we *are*," he does not act on this intuition. On the verge of an intellectual epiphany, Chandler understands that "the aesthetic impulse may thus be understood to be *moral*, and Nature, or life, is indeed, as Pope said, the *end* or purpose of Art. By this we mean that the highest state a man can achieve is one of *aesthetic wholeness* . . . the end of aesthetic evolution, *wholeness*, is analogous to the end of religious evolution, *saintliness*, that state in which one is capable of embracing all experience as holy and some experience as *more* holy" (202).

Such is the thrust of Gardner's theory of moral fiction. All of Gardner's protagonists journey toward this state of aesthetic wholeness in which they are able to affirm not just an individual conception of what one thinks life *means*, but all of what life *is*, "the *world*, the buzzing blooming confusion itself" (229). Yet Chandler's necessary epiphany has actually occurred much earlier, not as a result of his philosophical conceptualizing but as a result of a moment of pure intuition when he awakes one morning and stands looking out the window of his room:

8. *Encyclopedia of Philosophy*, ed. Paul Williams (8 vols.; New York, 1967), II, 143.

There lay before and around and within him a hundred different shades of green, a hundred different birdsongs, a thousand-thousand distinct, familiar shapes. One could understand, at moments like this, the great Romantic flight to Nature—the concern his mother and father had felt, and his mother felt still, if only from habit, with temperature and wind direction, or the concern that had sent two hundred years of painters like Aunt Emma scurrying to the trees.—Except, it came to him, that Aunt Emma's paintings had nothing to do with that. And then he knew all at once what it was in Aunt Emma's paintings, crude as they were, that gave one that sense of sudden release, unexpected joy, that one experienced in the presence of true works of art. And what was more, Chandler saw then, his heart tripping rapidly and lightly, with that one insight the whole aesthetic theory fell into place. She painted the soul's sublime acceptance of lawless, proliferating substance: things and their motions.
   A. A violent order is disorder; and
   B. A great disorder is an order. These
   Two things are one. (Pages of illustrations.) (166–67)

Rather than act upon this insight, Chandler remains immobilized by his need to systematize. Unable to accept the paradox of life revealed in these opening lines of Wallace Stevens' "Connoisseur of Chaos," Chandler attempts to incorporate the experience into his book as part of a theory or "system" of art. His problem, as it has been for all philosophers, is how to define and describe this intuitive knowledge in rational terms. In a sense, he encounters the same problem Gardner himself had, but never admitted, in putting his theory of fiction into the treatise form of *On Moral Fiction.* As Charles Johnson has commented, "[Gardner] asserted but he did not prove the priority of this perception [that fiction chooses the life-affirming vision above all others], because there can be no indubitable proof for such a claim. It is more a 'faith' than an argument, an appeal to hope that nags for systematic articulation, but which defies, at every turn, demonstration"[9] —except, Johnson adds, and I agree, through art itself, for the logic of philosophy is too limiting to communicate all that a "dramatization of ideas," art, can convey. Locked in such an impasse, Chandler, like all the artist/protagonists in Gardner's novels, needs the intervention of another person to break free of his limited vision and to make contact again with the world.

   Having used the example of Dante and Beatrice to explain the role of "saintly intercessor" in his novels, Gardner also discusses the need for such a person in terms of courtly love: "The lover does the most he

9. Charles Johnson, "A Phenomenology of *On Moral Fiction,*" in Henderson (ed.), *Thor's Hammer,* 153.

can possibly do, and then the grace of the lady saves him."[10] As we might expect, Gardner's intercessors are usually women of strength and compassion, like Chandler's wife Marie, but in contrast to what he does in later novels, Gardner ironically makes Chandler's savior the least saintly of the women in *The Resurrection*. Only Viola Staley's confession of love breaks Chandler finally from his need to conceptualize life: " 'I love you,' she whispered, terrified, pressing the side of her head to his cheek. She could not look at him until he answered, but waited in anguish for the heart on the altar to be taken or rejected" (224). Although Viola's gesture is melodramatic, the point, I think, is that she takes a chance on her feelings, offers them up to another human being despite the possibility of rejection.

The "sacrifice of her heart" saves Chandler, for confessing his need to be comforted and loved is an action he has stubbornly refused to take. Although Chandler at first rejects Viola's love and in doing so rejects an essential element that both frees and binds all of humanity, he realizes his failure soon after Viola leaves him in his mother's house. In one of the most significant passages in all of Gardner's work, Chandler understands that all along he has been rejecting what it is to be human, to exist as a part of the whole: "All this time it had been there right in front of him . . . and he'd missed it! It was not the beauty of the world one must affirm but *the world*, the buzzing blooming confusion itself. He had slipped from celebrating what was to the celebration of empty celebration . . . *One must make life art*" (229). With this knowledge, Chandler moves off to die at the feet of a strange young girl who loves him rather than among his immediate family. His final words, " 'No harm: It's done us no harm' " (232), take on a multitude of meanings, especially if considered in light of all of Gardner's novels, but the essence of the statement is that life, and death, do no harm. James Chandler learns, ironically, at the moment of his own death that all of life is worth affirming. Like Aunt Emma, he accepts himself and the world in "all of its lawless proliferation and decay" and achieves, if only momentarily, the sense of aesthetic wholeness for which he has been searching.

As well as the sacrificial love of an intercessor, each of Gardner's protagonists needs the strength derived from a gathering of the community in order to overcome the dilemma he faces. Such a gathering

10. Curt Suplee, "John Gardner, Flat Out," Washington *Post*, July 25, 1982, Sec. H, p. 8.

usually reminds the withdrawn protagonist that he is an integral part of the community and of society in general. In *The Resurrection*, however, James Chandler's time is so short that he is forced to choose between participating in the gathering for Elizabeth Staley's final annual recital and seeking out Viola Staley to ask for her blessing. Because Gardner has said the gathering at the recital provides "that closing of the circle, people clinging to each other and nourishing each other" when, especially for the Chandler family, "everything's gone horrible," at least one responsible critic of Gardner's work has taken Gardner's statements to mean that Chandler has failed in his attempt to achieve a vision of "aesthetic wholeness," that "the hope of resurrection is lost for James Chandler." Although such a reading seems supported by Gardner's statements that Chandler suffers from "cheap Platonism" and "does this wonderful self-sacrificing thing, which is in fact all wrong," I believe we cannot take Gardner's comments so literally without examining the ending of the novel more carefully, especially his use of the gathering, which is of such great importance in *Nickel Mountain, The Sunlight Dialogues*, and *October Light*.[11]

James Chandler does indeed cling to a "kind of easy idealism" throughout the novel, but in finally comprehending the sacrificial nature of Viola Staley's confession, he acts on faith and intuition. Such an action is at the very heart of Gardner's beliefs concerning the relationship between art and life, for as Chandler correctly argues, the separation of ethics and aesthetics is a mistake, and attempts at "intellectual metaphysics" are too limited to provide help with life. Chandler's logical metaphysical system may be a failure, but his action at the end of the novel, and at the end of his life, is, like art, life-affirming and true. His sacrifice is not empty because it is symbolic of what he has discovered about himself and the world, and it embodies an acceptance of death.

Chandler's decision to act occurs simultaneously with the gathering at the recital, his death perhaps simultaneously with the cacophony of *deaf* Aunt Betsy's piano-playing. As the recital begins, Gardner wants us to recall the lines from Stevens' "Connoisseur of Chaos," for out of the disorder of the "mindless [musical] roar of things and their motions" (243) comes a kind of order: "The people sat listening, perfectly silent, as if deeply impressed, staring at their knees" (244). In this

11. Ed Christian, "An Interview with John Gardner," *Prairie Schooner*, LIV (Winter, 1980–81), 74; Morris, *A World of Order and Light*, 37; Per Winther, "An Interview with John Gardner," *English Studies*, LXII (December, 1981), 515.

scene, suggestive of "The Emperor's New Clothes" (a child, Chandler's daughter, even cries out at what everyone else seems to ignore— " 'Mother, Miss Staley's *deaf*!' " [243-44]), Gardner reverses the moral of the fairy tale. Unlike the emperor's subjects, who ignore their leader's nakedness out of fear and foolishness, the community of Batavia is silent out of respect for Aunt Betsy and all that she has meant to them. The need for community, which Gardner emphasizes in all of his novels and especially in *Mickelsson's Ghosts*, is realized in his first published novel. While the innocent cry of a child in "The Emperor's New Clothes" exposes the hypocrisy of the community in appeasing its leader's vanity, the innocent observation of Chandler's daughter threatens to disrupt a truly important tribute by the community.

As Chandler dies, the whole community is coming together "at a moment of significance, the sad and splendid conclusion of an age," but everyone, including Chandler's wife and children, is also present at the beginning of a new age, a new order—"and whether or not they knew what it was they were witnessing, no stranger could have said" (244), because only those who are "of the community" can fully understand what they are witnessing. Chandler's final moments overcome his earlier disregard for family, for from among the "human family" —the community—he chooses perhaps the least worthy, Viola Staley, to whom he confesses his understanding of life and death. Chandler's death unites his family just as Aunt Betsy's recital unites the community. His family will be changed because of his tragic end, but just as Chandler has passed through all of the stages of dying, his family has passed through the initial stages of grief, so that at the moment of his death they are already beginning to create a new order symbolized by the coming together—the "healing of the wound," as Gardner called it—at which they are present.

The final exchanges between Chandler and Viola Staley are significant because indirectly they also free Chandler of his "ghost," Aunt Emma, when Viola goes to tell Chandler she loves him. Aunt Emma's forced confinement parallels Chandler's self-imposed isolation, and since her vision, in her art and in his dreams, moves Chandler toward his epiphany, it is fitting that, like the "ominous strangers and ghosts" in Gardner's novels which follow *The Resurrection*, she is freed by Chandler's unwitting intervention. Near the beginning of the novel, Gardner says of Chandler and Aunt Emma, "He saw her sitting erect and prim, waiting for a long-dead father or God? was that it?—waiting for *him*, whoever it was, to lead her away from the overpowering world of old mills and waterfalls and sundials of mossy stone" (67). At the end of the novel, we discover that Aunt Emma has been waiting for Chandler, not to lead her away from the world she once celebrated in her paintings but into it again.

James Chandler, as the "moral artist" in Gardner's first published novel, sets the pattern of rational and intuitive discovery for each of the protagonists of the novels that follow. Like Chandler, Gardner's artist/protagonists come to realize through a process of exploring and testing values that any attempt to impose an inflexible order on life results in stasis, a limited vision, and a lack of unity. Those characters who cling blindly to their own narrow conceptions of reality or to material representations of order are deemed "unfit for Nature" or "freaks of Nature" left to live out their lives in various states of isolation and despair. By ignoring the flux of the world, the wholeness of life, these characters become, by extension of metaphor, secondary or minor or failed artists whose art does not hold up with the passage of time because it constructs absolutes restricted by time and place rather than explores those values that are eternally human.

James Chandler's journey from a state of despair and indifference through a series of insights, sometimes violent and sometimes sublime, until he achieves an acceptance of the totality, the connectedness of things and his own feelings, and thereby the ability to understand the feelings and actions of others, establishes a precedent for the journeys of Gardner's other protagonists. Once they achieve this pinnacle of perception, they realize, as James Chandler does, the value of compassion, love, and forgiveness, and they see that by accepting the whole, including the process of change that is our world, they are offered each day the possibility of a new life, a new reality—a resurrection.

Mickelsson's Ghosts

In *Mickelsson's Ghosts*, John Gardner creates a work as broad in scope as *The Sunlight Dialogues* and returns to the explicit philosophical musings of *The Resurrection*. Gardner's prolific output has already resulted in four posthumous publications: two books of advice and instruction to prospective students and teachers of fiction writing, and two novels, *Stillness* and *Shadows*, the latter of which was said by Gardner to be "a summary of everything I've done, a recapitulation."[12] But Gardner's accidental death made *Mickelsson's Ghosts* the last novel he completed

12. Quoted in Morris, *A World of Order and Light*, 227.

for publication, and it seems to emphasize the full circle he apparently had already come in perfecting the kind of "energeic" novel in which he had so much faith.[13] Not only can we see a reiteration of the characters, thematic concerns, and plot of his first published novel, *The Resurrection*, in *Mickelsson's Ghosts* but also a shift in direction, the promise of what may have been a new and more varied approach to creating the "moral" or life-affirming fiction he so admired.

If James Chandler, the philosopher/protagonist of *The Resurrection*, had lived to achieve the fame and reputation he initially believes will make his life worthwhile, he would more than likely have arrived at the condition of Peter Mickelsson, the philosopher/protagonist of *Mickelsson's Ghosts*. "Burnt-out" is the handiest phrase to describe Mickelsson's state. Plagued with tax problems, separated from his wife and children, bored with the politics and drudgery of academic life at "Sunny," Mickelsson sweats away summer nights trying to "read, think, and write" in his shabby apartment in downtown Binghamton, New York.[14] Whereas James Chandler rushes to finish his new book on metaphysics because he believes it will somehow justify his limited span of existence on earth, Mickelsson, who has already achieved some degree of recognition, understands the brevity of fame and the lack of satisfaction it finally provides. United by the general disfavor of their specializations within the world of modern "analytical philosophy," Chandler as a metaphysician and Mickelsson as an ethician struggle not only to be heard above the din of twentieth-century commercialism and over-reliance on reason, but also to ameliorate the now "uninhabited castles of order" erected by great philosophers of the past. Although Chandler's early death saves him from the lingering depression and despair shared by Gardner's older protagonists, Mickelsson has descended very nearly into the "violence and madness" he is struggling to avoid: "Sometimes the feeling that his life was hopeless — and his misery to a large extent undeserved . . . would drive him down to the maple- or oak-lined streets at night, to prowl like a murderer" (5). Mickelsson's frustration and anger are revealed best by an early scene in which, acting instinctively, he bludgeons to death a neighborhood dog, a representation perhaps of the "unleashed" chaos of the world that Mickelsson wishes to obliterate from his life.

13. John Gardner, *The Art of Fiction* (New York, 1984), 185.
14. John Gardner, *Mickelsson's Ghosts* (New York, 1984), 5. Further references to this edition will be made in the text.

Shocked by his own senseless brutishness, Mickelsson, like Chandler, begins a desperate search for some meaning and order in his life. Having attached his depression to the place he inhabits, Mickelsson begins house-hunting, an activity that keeps him "just ahead of the shadow at his back, despair" (19). Following classified ads, he soon discovers in the mountains across the Pennsylvania border an old farmhouse that arouses his attachment to the past: "It stirred in him memories, at first only a general mood—exhilaration . . . and then, all at once, a specific moment: running naked, as a boy, in his father's overgrown apple orchard" (20). The Edenic imagery is obvious, and Mickelsson's association of the farmhouse with this pastoral vision of boyhood strengthens his feeling that the house and farm may hold the peace and solitude he needs. The house, of course, offers an escape as well as a possibility for positive change: "he felt himself hovering on the brink of something, as if the stubborn will by means of which he'd survived his troubles were at last getting ready to pay off" (20). Following the pattern familiar to readers of Gardner's novels, Mickelsson retreats from the city into the beautiful yet forbidding natural world. At the same time, in the fashion shared by Gardner's other protagonists who reach impasses in their lives, Mickelsson withdraws even further into himself. Like James Chandler, who retreats to his childhood home of Batavia, New York, Mickelsson first looks to his own past of rural living and hard work in hopes of restoring some order and stability to his life. Mickelsson's farmhouse receives the force of this desire to return to such a past, and soon becomes a symbol not only of Mickelsson's distant and recent past but also of the connectedness of humanity over the ages.

On the very first night he spends in the farmhouse, Mickelsson begins to meditate on the natural world and its associations with the past. Most notably in *October Light*, Gardner reveals the easy attraction of the past as resting in traditional values; obviously, most people prefer to embrace established values—"the good old days"—rather than work to reevaluate and reformulate those values in light of present conditions. Yet it is the testing of such values that Gardner believes is so important in art and life. Mickelsson's withdrawal into the countryside of Susquehanna County allows him to escape the stale routine of the city but also seduces him into an even deeper and more threatening isolation than he has yet experienced.

Mickelsson's house reminds him of the comforts of life with his wife and two children and with his own father, mother, and uncle, but it also contains a past of its own, which is revealed in the stories Mickelsson hears about its ghosts from local residents and in what Mickelsson eventually comes to believe are his own psychic visions.[15] The ghosts of the house, both those that inhabit the place and those Mickelsson brings with him, are the "ominous strangers" of the novel, possessing information Mickelsson needs in order to work his way out of isolation and stasis. At first Mickelsson is haunted only by his personal past, but when he begins to see and talk not only to the ghosts of the old couple who lived and suffered in the house but also to the ghosts of long-dead philosophers, we understand that the house has come to represent a historical past as well. Through Mickelsson, who treads a narrow ledge above the abyss of madness, Gardner develops the house into a symbol of time's continuum—"all at once . . . he was seeing the whole history of the house: weddings, funerals, births, deaths, battles" (132). To some extent the extensive philosophical monologues and dialogues, for which many reviewers have condemned the novel, are Mickelsson's mind-wrenching attempts to reconcile the past he admires with the modern world he so despises. In clinging to his house and to the "natural" and intellectual life of the past, Mickelsson rejects all city and community—that is, all modern—values.

Just as Nickel, Crow, and Prospect mountains become islands of refuge surrounded by the natural world in *Nickel Mountain* and *October Light*, so Mickelsson's house is an island surrounded by the natural world of the Endless Mountains. His attraction to this environment is strong, and to a certain degree the natural world and its people provide an atmosphere conducive to renewal, as Gardner makes apparent in all of his novels. Initially, Mickelsson's retreat is uplifting, and as he adapts the old farmhouse to his own tastes, he makes brief attempts to reenter the mainstream of life. He has a Christmas party for fellow faculty and begins a relationship with sociology professor Jessica Stark, and he recalls how the long stretches of days in the Adirondacks used to renew his vision and lead to seemingly easy philosophizing: "It had never seemed to him there that the world was a cypher. . . . There the world was itself, as immediate as his thought, his huge, nameless desires. Back in the camp he would write essays, chapters, explanations and speculations with the carefree delight of a child lost in fantasy" (481). The environment of the Endless Mountains, he

---

15. See Jeff Henderson, "John Gardner's Layered Fiction: The Supernatural and the Paranatural," in Henderson (ed.), *Thor's Hammer*, 167–80, for an excellent discussion of "ghosts" in Gardner's novels.

hopes, will restore the ease with which he was once able to think and write, but Mickelsson's obsession with the house and the past it represents blinds him to the need for maintaining more than casual contact with humanity. His decision to cut himself off from Binghamton makes him akin to James Page and George Loomis, both of whom cling desperately to their houses and farms as material representations of an order that has all but vanished. Unlike Page and Loomis, however, Mickelsson has an intimation of the finality to which a retreat of the kind he has chosen leads.

Although the natural world promises, and sometimes allows, certain freedoms and flights of fancy, it also always contains, as Gardner reminds us in his fiction, the horror and darkness of death. Mickelsson soon realizes that his retreat into the rural world of Susquehanna is a desperate and perhaps fatal last grasp at nonexistent possibilities. The beautiful natural world contains the indifference and randomness of the evolutionary process at work and provides a convenient means for hiding the dumping of toxic wastes that have poisoned several residents, including perhaps Mickelsson himself. An even worse fate, however, seems to be in store for Mickelsson. On the verge of mental incapacitation, he faces a kind of living death created by his isolation from humanity. Michael Nugent, one of Mickelsson's students and another of the information-carrying "ghosts" who "haunt" Mickelsson in the novel, confronts Mickelsson with the darker side of his retreat: " 'All I meant,' Nugent said, watching his face, 'is, everybody hates it that the modern world's so civilized and boring and generally safe, so crushing to the human soul and imagination. Everybody wants to get back to simplicity. . . . Nobody has the faintest understanding of, well, you know, the *awful* part, the perdurable evils' " (106–107). Although warned by Nugent and acknowledging his own intuition that "the soul in isolation, no matter what the stimulation of the world around, would shrivel up, like a plant perfectly healthy except for its signal leaf, and die" (213), Mickelsson nevertheless presses on with his restoration of the house to the exclusion of all else in his life. Eventually, he no longer even bothers to return to Binghamton to teach.

In choosing to remain isolated, Mickelsson also rejects the "saving" love of Jessica Stark, one of the intercessors of *Mickelsson's Ghosts*. Like the old Vermont farmer James Page, who is shocked to realize he still has the capacity to love, Mickelsson understands his feelings for Jessica but sees them as a kind of betrayal of his logical yet nihilistic view of the world—a view reinforced by his ghostly companions Martin Luther and Friedrich Nietzsche. After spending two nights with her at his farmhouse as Jessica tries to help him reorder the chaos of his financial situation and lighten the emotional baggage of his separation from his wife and children, Mickelsson is suddenly "absolutely sure that she did indeed love him" (239), but his reason keeps telling him that such feelings, for him at least, are "bullshit" (270). Unable to admit that acting on positive human emotions is as justifiable a way to live as relying solely on rational decision-making processes, Mickelsson, like his fellow philosopher James Chandler, is torn between abstractions of reality and the world itself. Mickelsson shuts off the only true means of seeking truth—a balanced combination of reason, imagination, and human interaction. The importance of this critical ingredient of interaction—love—is emphasized throughout Gardner's fiction, but especially in this novel. When another of Mickelsson's students, an antithesis of the dour Nugent, suggests that true values are discovered in " 'maybe the wisdom of the whole community, like, tested over time' " (185), Mickelsson scoffs. Despite his rejection of "eternal verities" as the only lasting system of ethics, Mickelsson does sense his own pathetic plight: "A man was never more alone, he thought, than when standing by himself looking at the lights of a community across a river, or across a lake, or from the deck of a ship" (236); and "he could not entirely drive from his consciousness the strangeness of what he was doing, fixing the place up when he had no one but himself to do it for" (212). Although Mickelsson may be somewhat frightened by what he thinks of as Jessica's "unique" embodiment of intelligence and beauty, it is only through sheer, stubborn will—a refusal to come to grips with his own feelings and prejudices— that he sinks into the more comfortable but isolated routine of restoring his farmhouse and into a less-demanding but guilt-ridden relationship with Susquehanna's town whore.

Although Jessica Stark's love will eventually draw Mickelsson back into the world he has temporarily rejected, the comfort of Donnie Matthews' easy sexuality probably saves Mickelsson from insanity by providing a release for the emotions and physical desires he keeps locked up during his "retreat." Susquehanna's young prostitute seems to act as a counterpoint to the sophisticated and intelligent Jessica Stark and is, like Viola Staley, an unusual version of Gardner's saintly intercessor. Mickelsson's love-making with Donnie liberates him to a certain extent, though the feeling does not last beyond a momentary euphoria that accompanies the physical act, and because she is about the age of his daughter, Donnie also adds to Mickelsson's guilt and suffering. Nevertheless, his relationship with her does move him into a union with the small community and eventually back to Jessica and the world at large: "For all his misery, guilt, and dread, he was beginning to feel like a native of sorts" (452).

When he accidentally causes the death of the old, fat bank robber (who lives in Susquehanna but is not a part of the community) while stealing the man's cache for Donnie's abortion, the people of the town forgive him. Ironically, Mickelsson's confession of guilt is met with the very communal value system that he has secretly admired but consciously rejected: " 'You can get away with a lot here . . . if the town likes you,' " he is told; " 'it's not so much the laws on the books that people care about, in Susquehanna' " (509). By becoming involved with Donnie, and perhaps by impregnating her, Mickelsson—who until this point has been overwhelmed by entropy—finds himself arguing *for* life in spite of its seeming brutishness and pointlessness. Stuck at an impasse—"the world is shit," "God is dead," "even suicide is empty rhetoric"—and waiting for "some miracle, some burst of illuminating, all-transforming light out of Heaven" (342), Mickelsson is finally forced to act when Donnie insists on having an abortion. His desire to preserve the fetus' life and his subsequent accidental killing of the fat robber, coming as they do from an emotional outbust rather than from a calculated philosophical argument or plan, jar Mickelsson into contact with humanity and out of his isolated state. If nothing else, he is drawn into the cover-up perpetuated by local authorities and begins to understand that it is "better to act with fully conscious stupidity" (403) than to do nothing at all and become a victim of stasis.

After the death of the fat man and Donnie's disappearance from town, Mickelsson returns to his house and actually moves toward a significant understanding of his life, the kind of all-encompassing vision Gardner's protagonists usually achieve. Mickelsson begins to see the limitations of logic and of adherence to a philosophical system in establishing some form of order amid the chaos of life: "Perhaps the whole thing had to do with . . . a commonplace these days—the lack of connection between head and heart, the abyss between belief and attitude, cognitive and conative" (421). The meeting between Mickelsson and his daughter, which reveals her love for him despite what he sees as his betrayal of her through the separation from her mother, provides another jolt toward acceptance of his human limitations and the knowledge that feelings as well as reason can provide answers in the search for values: "How long had he been like this, blind, insensitive as a stone, casually murderous. . . . Perhaps the fact that he could feel shame at what he'd become was a sign that there was hope" (470). It would be joyous to believe in a didactic truth or a system of absolutes, as the Marxists in Jessica Stark's department do or as the Nazis did before them, Mickelsson thinks, but it would also "be moronic" (447). Like James Chandler, Mickelsson discovers that writing a "big book on philosophy" as a means of reordering life and reentering the world cannot compare to embracing the simple yet universal feelings of love, compassion, and sympathy.

Unsure of where to turn in the face of the revelations brought on by his acceptance in the community of Susquehanna, his involvement and break-up with Donnie Matthews, and his meeting with his daughter, Mickelsson returns to his only source of security at the moment—his house: "Even now, in his hopelessness and guilt, he could not deny that his knowledge of the house around him, restored by his hands to something like its former beauty, miraculously cleaned up like the world of Noah, gave a kind of security, however tentative; a place to stand" (475). In keeping with his own technique of manipulating what Melville called "the ambiguities," Gardner makes the house into the source of Mickelsson's painful isolation from the world but at the same time the source of Mickelsson's final movements toward reintegration.

In stimulating Mickelsson to rediscover his own past and to commune with the dead philosophers he admires (and hates), the house becomes the touchstone Mickelsson needs in order to revaluate his life. Mickelsson's obsession with the ominous ghosts of Luther and Nietzsche has to do with their antithetical views of life. In *Freddy's Book*, Gardner has said, he worked out the conflict between these two philosophers, and his explanation goes a long way toward revealing Mickelsson's attempts to recover stability in his life. Mickelsson shares Luther's "devilish" belief that "all life is . . . shit" and that "there is no possibility of good works because people are such creeps." But since "Luther's Christian world is dead," Gardner says, Mickelsson cannot bring himself to place his faith only in Luther's "salvation through grace." At this point, Gardner creates a certain irony in Mickelsson's thinking. Mickelsson rejects the modern world by retreating to the pastoral confines of Susquehanna, but like most inhabitants of the modern world, Mickelsson seems to insist on Nietzsche's alternative to "salvation through grace"—"save yourself." Mickelsson's attempt at sublimation, however, becomes "a vicious circle," for the farther he retreats from reality the more cynical he becomes and the less able to see that, in Donne's phrase, "no man is an island." The question for Mickelsson, as for Freddy Agaard, is "how much can he save himself and how much does he need other people."[16]

Mickelsson eventually comes to realize that the "superman" does exist, but in a version far different than Nietzsche's: "men who, like Mickelsson's father, had given up thought long ago: men who simply acted—not out of pity but with infallible faith and love" (476). The guidance of such faith and love, Gardner says in *On Becoming a Novelist*, is an integral part of the moral artist's nature, and, as Peter Mickelsson gradually understands, these verities will allow him to transcend the moment and restructure his life. The rehabilitated farmhouse is a work of art in itself, and Mickelsson's model artist turns out to be not the great philosophers of despair but the simple carpenter and farmer—his own father. Mickelsson's father worked on their house to please Mickelsson's mother, a Beatrice of her time, and Mickelsson works on his house to recreate a similar atmosphere, one in which precious sacrifices were made, appreciated, and returned. Although the house, its ghosts, and its pastoral surroundings offer insight and inspiration to Mickelsson, they cannot provide the flexibility and lasting worth of bonds of emotion with real people in the present moment. Eventually, Gardner suggests, the past must be compromised with or adapted to the present. Mickelsson can only go so far in reconciling the views of Luther and Nietzsche, for he requires, as Gardner suggests in all of his novels, an intercessor.

In his confrontation with Lawler, the murdering, radical Mormon —another example of "systematic living" taken to the extreme—Mickelsson is finally forced to make a choice: he must destroy his house bit by bit with a wrecking bar or he must give up his own life. If he destroys the house, he sacrifices all of those associations with the past that it has held for him as well as the actual labor and sweat that have gone into its remodeling. If he chooses to die, he will be sacrificing perhaps the only thing worth living for—life itself. Although he does not realize it in the agony of the moment, Mickelsson, by destroying his house, turns away from the past, which is but a ghostly illusion, inflexible and static in time, toward an affirmation of his life in the pres-

16. Beatrice Mendez-Engle (ed.), *John Gardner: True Art, Moral Art,* Living Author Series No. 5 (Edinburg, Tex., 1983), 99.

ent, in spite of its confusion and pain.[17] Mickelsson's silent cry for help, a cry that transforms him and reconnects him with the human community, seems to banish his ghosts. Unlike George Loomis, who at the end of *Nickel Mountain* retreats with ghosts of the past to his dark isolated house on the mountain, Mickelsson rejoins the human community. His friends in Susquehanna answer his cry for help, taking care of him during his recovery and repairing some of the damage done to his house. The gathering of the community around him literally saves Mickelsson's life, but he has yet to move toward reunion with the world at large.

Mickelsson's return to Binghamton and Jessica Stark suggests a turning away from the specific kind of resolution encountered in what I loosely refer to as Gardner's "realistic" novels — those in modern settings and times. Although the usual pattern Gardner has established leads through a series of discoveries and minor setbacks toward the protagonist's eventual reintegration, *Mickelsson's Ghosts* does not arrive at such a clear resolution. James Chandler learns to celebrate "the world, in all its buzzing blooming confusion," Henry Soames discovers "the holiness of things . . . the idea of magical change," Fred Clumly is borne up "to where the light was brighter than sun-filled clouds, disanimated, and holy," and James Page's "blackened heart is melted." At no point, however, in *Mickelsson's Ghosts* do Mickelsson's dark visions and doubts seem to be so surely lifted. Some breakthroughs occur, suggesting resolution is possible, yet no certain revelation appears, unless the final scene of the novel — Mickelsson's sexual union with Jessica and the rainfall of souls — can be seen in such a light. Even so, Mickelsson's grasp of the importance of what may be happening in this scene, whether he has lost his hold on sanity or not, is not made apparent, leaving the reader with a sense that something significant has taken place but unsure of what it may mean to Mickelsson and those around him. Two important similarities between the endings of *The Resurrection* and *Mickelsson's Ghosts* are obvious. Mickelsson, like James Chandler, seeks out the woman to whom he believes his confession of love will mean the most, both for himself and for her, and both novels end with the gathering of friends and family so integral to all of Gardner's protagonists. While Chandler seems aware that he has reached some understanding of life and death, however, Mickelsson's thoughts

---

17. See Cowart, *Arches and Light*, 188-204, for a different view of Gardner's attitude toward the past.

on whether or not he has achieved the order and stability for which he has been searching are unclear.

Briefly, in the last pages of the novel, Mickelsson puts on his red hunting coat, which he wore when he had a mental breakdown earlier in his life, and goes to a party in progress at Jessica Stark's house. Caught up, the partygoers believe, in his own madness, Mickelsson confesses his love for Jessica, and they engage in sexual intercourse in the bedroom while all of the world—the greatest of Gardner's gatherings— appears to watch. As the party continues in the next room, outside the house "bones were tumbling onto the lawn, clattering in the street, booming like falling boulders, dropping out of nowhere" (589).

> Now the bedroom was packed tight with ghosts, not just people but also animals—minks, lynxes, foxes—more than Mickelsson or Jessie could name, and there were still more at the windows, oblivious to the tumbling, roaring bones and blood, the rumbling at the door, though some had their arms or paws over their heads—both people and animals, an occasional bird, still more beyond, some of them laughing, some looking away (Mormons, Presbyterians), some blowing their noses and brushing away tears, some of them clasping their hands or paws and softly mewing, shadowy cats, golden-eyed tigers (Marxist atheists, mournful Catholics) . . . pitiful, empty-headed nothings complaining to be born. (590)

What may appear to be a final drifting into madness caused by Mickelsson's physically and mentally exhausting encounter with Lawler may actually be a more subtle revelation of the protagonist's achievement of renewal than Gardner has previously attempted. After all, Mickelsson, mad or not, does choose to return to the city, to Jessica, and to humanity.

The problem, if it is one, is that Gardner's "realistic" novels are usually very direct in portraying the final resolutions of their artist/protagonists' crises. Such directness is justified by Gardner through his belief that art is not "a mirror of life" and fiction should not be a loose rabble of ideas but a firmly constructed work in which ideas, values, feelings, and beliefs are tested and reevaluated, with the best affirmed and passed on to the reader.[18] Nevertheless, after the "sound and fury" accompanying publication of *On Moral Fiction*, Gardner's novels become more subtle and mysterious in providing satisfying resolutions and, as some critics have suggested, in making direct replies to those who attacked *On Moral Fiction*. Although humanity is victorious over "the Devil" in *Freddy's Book* and the moral artist's (Freddy's)

18. Gardner, *On Moral Fiction*, 14.

vision is affirmed, the novel apparently leaves readers wondering about Jack Winesap, who, though he possesses characteristics typical of Gardner's protagonists, never so much as comments on what he learns from Freddy's novella. Gardner has stated emphatically that he never intended to return to Winesap, that the "Freddy" portion of the novel acts in the same way as Hawthorne's "The Custom House" prelude does in *The Scarlet Letter*; nevertheless, *Freddy's Book* still seems to leave readers puzzled. *Mickelsson's Ghosts* intimately parades the trials and tribulations of Peter Mickelsson for nearly six hundred pages, ending with a very moving and somewhat celebratory scene, yet reviewers expressed the same sense of dissatisfaction with *Mickelsson's Ghosts* as they did with *Freddy's Book*.

Although one could argue that a resolution is apparent in *Mickelsson's Ghosts*, it is largely dependent upon the established pattern of Gardner's previous novels, and it is hardly as direct as in Gardner's work before *On Moral Fiction* was published. For instance, Mickelsson's "madness," which all of Gardner's protagonists possess to some degree, may be interpreted as a kind of joyous innocence or a hysterical celebration of life in the midst of a community celebration such as we see evolving out of gatherings in *Nickel Mountain* and *October Light*. The rain of souls — people and animals — parallels the kind of exorcism of the past represented by the ghosts disappearing at the end of *Nickel Mountain*. At the same time, the souls "complaining to be born" may suggest that the desire for life, in all of its horror and joy, is stronger than any other feeling that human beings and animals possess and is the only value truly worth affirming in the past, present, and future — an argument on which Gardner's children's novella *In The Suicide Mountains* is based. *Mickelsson's Ghosts* also further develops the characterization and philosophizing of Mickelsson's colleague James Chandler in *The Resurrection*.

Three specific characteristics of Gardner's last novel, however, suggest more than the simple "falling off" in his work that even critics friendly to Gardner's work have offered as explanation for the "failure" of *Mickelsson's Ghosts*. Gardner's use of a limited third-person point of view in the novel is an intriguing exception to his prejudice against limiting the narrative point of view, and one wonders if Gardner abandoned his narrative principles to some extent in order to create a different perspective of his protagonist's struggle, one that, because of its claustrophobic nature, might throw "moral fiction hunters" off the track. Using the graphically described sex act, which we do not see in any other novel, as a symbol of union, or reunion, with the world represented by Jessica Stark and the people at the party in her house is certainly a new tactic for Gardner and may obscure his usual philosophical resolution. And the deliberate ambiguity of the ending of the novel, when considered in light of the combination of "realistic" and "fabulistic" story lines of *Freddy's Book*, is perhaps an attempt to move the "realistic" novels closer toward the ambiguity of the "fabulistic" novels—those set in some time removed from the twentieth century. I believe the lack of a clear resolution in *Mickelsson's Ghosts* suggests a transition in Gardner's approach or thinking, especially since in none of his other novels with modern settings and times—*The Resurrection, Nickel Mountain, The Sunlight Dialogues, October Light*—does he hedge on matter-of-fact resolutions. The ending of *Mickelsson's Ghosts* suggests the creation of a closer link between Gardner's "realistic" and "fabulistic" novels. Because of his untimely death, however, we will never know to what this transition may have led.

2
Nature as Moral Center
Nickel Mountain
and *October Light*

The *process* of writing becomes more and more
mysterious as you go over the draft more and
more times. . . . Frequently, when you write a
novel you start out feeling pretty clear about
your position, what side you're on; as you
revise, you find your unconscious pushing up
associations that modify that position, force you
to reconsider. —JOHN GARDNER

Nickel Mountain

In *The Resurrection* and *Mickelsson's Ghosts* Gardner creates philosophers who attempt to establish an intellectual basis for his theory of
moral fiction. In *Nickel Mountain* and *October Light*, however, he
uses the emotional Henry Soames and laconic James Page to *dramatize* the theory. Henry Soames, owner of the Stop-Off cafe halfway up
Nickel Mountain, is a man of uncontrollable feelings. His journey toward a vision akin to aesthetic wholeness is by means of intuitive ac-
knowledgments of the changing nature of his life and of the world
around him. Like James Chandler, he is threatened with death, but
unlike Chandler, he is closely atuned to the world in which he lives.
His meditations upon the landscape of the Catskills recur at key decision-making instances throughout the novel. Because he is a careful
observer of the processes of nature, Henry is open-minded in the face
of change and is able to adapt more readily than Chandler to his
changing situation and the fluctuating social conditions of the world.

In creating "A Pastoral Novel," as *Nickel Mountain* is subtitled,
Gardner confines the setting to a community of people with direct relationships to the land and emphasizes that the harried life of the city
allows people neither the time nor the patience to understand fully
themselves and others around them. The rural setting, as Gregory

Morris has pointed out, strips away much of the superficial complexity of urban life that obscures the underlying problems confronting each of us. The clutter of modern urban life, Gardner also believes, either automatizes or disillusions people. Henry Soames, for instance, is appalled to think of some old man "stabbed in New York City" while fifteen people stood by without interfering or even calling the police: "A man could turn into an animal, then. It was something about living in the city, that was all he could figure. . . . He'd felt it himself one time in Utica. He'd never have believed there were that many people in all this world, especially that many poor people, burnt-out-looking . . . faces that stared right through him." Both George Loomis and Willard Freund, natives of the Catskills, leave their homes only to return bitter, hardened, and disillusioned with life. The pastoral heights of Nickel Mountain stand in contrast to the towns and cities of the valleys, and the values of human interaction with the small rural community are celebrated throughout the novel. That Henry Soames rises out of his state of despair is due not only to his own perceptiveness and good judgment but also to his environment and to the concern of his friends and family.[1]

As well as establishing the city/country contrast in *Nickel Mountain*, Gardner takes pains to show that rural life is more conducive to maintaining human contact and a sense of community. *Nickel Mountain* is faithful to the pastoral novel as a genre, but Gardner, as always, examines the inevitable change taking place in the rural world. With television (which comes under more direct attack in *October Light*) and other forms of mass communication, urban values are broadcast into the most isolated hamlets. Thus *Nickel Mountain* and *October Light* differ from Gardner's other novels in their emphasis on "perceivers" over "thinkers" and in the pattern of retreat and discovery the protagonists follow. Henry Soames and James Page do not have to retreat into nature, for they, somewhat like Grendel, have never left it. As pastoral novels, *Nickel Mountain* and *October Light* "reveal the moral value of a small community of persons living next to the land, sharing the burdens of labor and the hours of leisure," but these novels also raise questions about how much of the moral value of such a community is worth pre-

---

1. Samuel Coale, " 'Into the Farther Darkness': The Manichean Pastoralism of John Gardner," in Robert A. Morace and Kathryn VanSpanckeren (eds.), *John Gardner: Critical Perspectives* (Carbondale, Ill., 1982), 15–27; John Gardner, *Nickel Mountain* (New York, 1973), 179. Further references to this edition will be made in the text.

serving. The Stop-Off itself is a place like Melville's ships or Cooper's borderlands, suspended between the depths of nature and the artificiality of civilization. Gardner uses the rural community around the Stop-Off, as he also uses the small Vermont farming community in *October Light*, to test the traditional moral values established by the experience of years of intimacy with the natural world.[2]

Henry Soames's initial state of despair results from the self-pity and hatred of the "sentimental Soames blood" he has inherited from his father. A grotesquely fat mountain of a man, Henry embodies all of his father's elephantine bulk as well as his highly emotional temperament. These physical and emotional characteristics have made Henry's life miserable and now, by weakening his heart, threaten to end it altogether. He yearns to be free of such an inheritance, "for well as Henry Soames knew who he was, the idea that a man might be somebody else all his life and never be aware of it—live out the wrong doom, grow fat because a man he had nothing to do with by blood had died of fat —had a strange way of filling up his chest. In bed sometimes he would think about it . . . merely savoring the immense half-possibility" (15). Henry's escapes from what seems genetically determined are his wild rides up Nickel Mountain in his '39 Ford: "On a clear night you could make it to the top of Nickel Mountain and back, teetering in the square black Ford, the walls pinning you in like the sides of an up-ended coffin, bumping down gravel and macadam roads and over the warped planks of narrow bridges that rocked when you hit and echoed *brrrack*! through the hills and glens. The trees would slide into the headlight beams and the wind whipping through the open window made you feel like Jesus H. Christ charioting to heaven" (31).

The irony of Henry's predicament lies in this casual association with Christ. Henry is described as "drunk from the huge, stupid love of Man that moved through his mind on its heels, empty and meaningless as fog, a Love of Man that came down in the end to wanting the whole damn world to itself, an empty diner, sticky places on the counter stools, bolts and old wrenches, sheer pins, cotter-keys, baling wire up to your knees on the floor of the garage" (31). Yet he is ashamed of his love of humanity, of the world at large, and associates his feelings with his father's "womanish" nature. As Gardner has noted, Henry's monstrous physical appearance contains "monstrous emotions . . . he really is a monster and he's holding it in, and that makes him human." Henry's

2. Michael Squires, *The Pastoral Novel: Studies in George Eliot, Thomas Hardy, and D. H. Lawrence* (Charlottesville, Va., 1974), 15, 16.

"monstrousness" arises partly from his own inability to deal with the "surfeit of emotion that warps his behavior and that overshadows his reliable intuitive sense," as Gregory Morris notes. But Henry's despair and anger are only increased when his attempts to communicate with others on an intimate level are rebuffed. He is made more ashamed of his feelings by the obvious uneasiness of people to whom he tries to express himself: "People shied from you when you tried to get to them, talk of a wife's sickness, a jackknifed truck, hoping to make them feel at home" (30). As a result of his inability to perceive any value in the temperament he has inherited from his father and to communicate his feelings for others, Henry's frustration manifests itself in the rage that Gardner's protagonists always feel. Even Henry's friends wonder about his sanity when he "roared up Nickel Mountain" or "pounded on the counter about the weather." What they do not realize is that they are partially responsible for his "madness."[3]

When Henry's rage is spent, he can only shake his head in wonder: " 'It's a funny damn world.' He would turn and squint out the window a while, trying to think about it, sensing the profundity of it but unable to find the words to express it even to himself. Vague images would come: children, trees, dogs, red brick houses, people he knew. He felt nothing; a heaviness only, a numbness in the chest" (5). Henry's inability to accept his own physical condition and emotional tirades as parts of his nature—what Collingwood would call an inability to transform feeling into language—prevents him from achieving the wholeness or balance that would lighten his anguish. As Henry struggles with his despair, he becomes very much like one of the postmodern artists Gardner condemns in *On Moral Fiction*. Henry "looks into his heart and sees chaos there, and denies, forever after, that one mode of action is better than another for senseless, purposeless humanity."[4] Until he is able to comprehend that the world and his place in it are neither "funny" nor "damned" but merely "are," he will not be able to see "the holiness of all things" that an artist's aesthetically whole vision can reveal.

When Henry is not raging against his situation or rocketing up Nickel Mountain to escape it, he tends to meditate upon his life, the lives of the people he knows, and his relationship to them. As these meditations reveal, Henry possesses the necessary imagination and will to change his life, for Gardner believes there is an alternative to

3. Morris, *A World of Order and Light*, 99–100.
4. Gardner, *On Moral Fiction*, 24.

the "fight or flight" syndrome aroused in us by the despair of modern life. Similarly, an artist with the necessary imagination may be able to consider a more desirable and inclusive vision than the nihilism into which so many recent artists have fallen:

> Leo Tolstoy knew about the universe of despair and endured a perhaps similar spiritual crisis, a crisis certainly profound and all-transforming. He came out of it not with a theory that every man should make up his own rules, asserting values for all men for all time, but with a theory of submission, a theory which equally emphasized freedom but argued that what a man ought to do with his freedom is be quiet, look and listen, try to feel out in his heart and bones what God requires of him—as Levin does in *Anna Karenina*, or Pierre in *War and Peace*. For God, if you wish, read "sympathy, empathy, scrupulous study of the everyday world and the best men's books."[5]

In *Nickel Mountain*, Henry Soames lacks the "best men's books," but he is completely involved in studying the everyday world from his vantage point behind the counter in the Stop-Off, and despite his "violent streak," he is often engaged in the quiet looking and listening of Gardner's moral artist. As Henry gradually accepts his feelings and intuitions as guides to action, he begins to be less ashamed of himself and to understand that his need for interaction with others is a universal one.

Gardner's use of the natural correlations of human character and mind is a means of allowing the reader to comprehend what Henry Soames feels and perceives of himself and of others. On the opening page of the novel, the description of what Henry sees outside the window of the Stop-Off reveals the state of his mind and heart:

> Sometimes when he was not in a mood to read he would stand at the window and watch the snow. On windy nights the snow hurtled down through the mountain's darkness and into the blue-white glow of the diner and the pink glitter of the neon sign and away again into the farther darkness and the woods on the other side of the highway. Henry Soames would pull at his lip with his thumb and first finger, vaguely afraid of the storm and vaguely drawn by it. He would imagine shapes in the snow that shot past, mainly his own huge, lumbering shape, but sometimes that of some ominous stranger. (3)

The isolation of the Stop-Off, the cold darkness, the storm, all reflect Henry's physical and mental despair: "His heart was bad, business at the Stop-Off had never been worse, he was close to a nervous breakdown" (3). Henry projects his own "lumbering shape" into the snow because he is lost in the storm of his feelings. More important, how-

5. *Ibid.*, 25–26.

ever, is Henry's association of his image in the snow with that of "some ominous stranger." Like the intruder of *The Resurrection*, who appears threatening but offers the knowledge James Chandler needs, the "ominous stranger" comes again and again to Henry Soames until he grasps its significance. Specifically, the appearance of the stranger at the beginning of the novel foreshadows the arrivals of those people who will move into and alter Henry's life: Callie, her baby Jimmy, and Simon Bale. Because it arises out of the natural world, the stranger or intruder image in *Nickel Mountain* also seems to represent the life force, or what Wordsworth calls "something far more deeply interfused." Gardner, in fact, quotes from "Tintern Abbey" in both *October Light* and *On Moral Fiction*, and as in all of his novels, the ominous stranger — "a motion and a spirit, that impels/All thinking things, all objects of all thought" — represents knowledge that must be accepted and expressed by the artist/protagonist in his art/life to enable him to carry on.

The winter imagery out of which Henry's shape and the ominous stranger appear dominates the first half of the book and is primarily associated with Henry's initial dormant condition. " 'You can't teach an old dog new tricks,' " Henry says of himself. But his relationship with young Callie Wells makes a lie of the cliché. Henry's despair is lessened by the love he feels for Callie when she comes to work at the Stop-Off. As one of Gardner's intercessors, Callie is associated with the rebirth or grace she helps to make possible for Henry. In Callie's case, the associations are very direct. She enters Henry's life "like a crocus where yesterday there'd been snow" (7), and the stirrings of affection in Henry are attributed to the change in the weather that accompanies her arrival: "the smell that had been in the air all week of wet, gray-brown hillsides coming to life, roots stirring, trees budding someplace to the south" (7–8). Callie's association with spring carries a literal significance as well, for she will soon give birth.

Callie's understanding of Henry's emotional outbursts, or at least her tolerance of them, allows him a different perspective on his "inheritance," for "she seemed for the most part not to mind, or rather to forgive, the weak, sentimental Soames in his blood" (28). The next time Henry ascends Nickel Mountain, he finds himself "not little Fats and not Henry Soames but someone who had been cold and dead for a long time" (46). The stirrings of a resurrection are apparent, for Callie awakens new possibilities in Henry, and the image he has of himself begins to change under the influence of her love. When Willard

Freund leaves Callie pregnant, the marriage between Henry and Callie and the birth of her son further open Henry's eyes to elements of change in the world, and these universal rituals infuse his life with new responsibility and interdependence.

Some critics have misunderstood Gardner's elaborate use of marriage and birth rituals in *Nickel Mountain.* Gardner does not embrace the rituals themselves, but uses them to develop the theme that people need to celebrate life itself rather than abstract ideals and ideas about life. The rituals of marriage and birth (and death) in Gardner's novels usually create the gathering of family and friends necessary to further the protagonists' testing of values. The family, Gardner suggests (and family is always a microcosm for community, as community is a microcosm for humanity in Gardner's fiction), is an individual's most intimate link with the ultimate human feeling—love. "Great art," Gardner has said, "celebrates life's potential, offering a vision unmistakably and unsentimentally rooted in love."[6] This powerful feeling, which in Gardner's work unites human beings against darkness, is also apparent in his development of characters. In the same way that Gardner's protagonists must be drawn from their isolation by love for others, the moral artist must love all of his creations—all people—enough to portray them sympathetically. Even Gardner's grotesque characters—Viola Staley, John Horne, Simon Bale—share a common humanity with the reader.

As an artist, Gardner shows compassion for his characters, and compassion for others is exactly what James Chandler, Henry Soames, Fred Clumly, and the rest of Gardner's protagonists must develop in order to accept themselves and their world completely. Gardner agrees with Shelley that "the great secret of morals is Love; or a going out of our own nature, and an identification of ourselves with the beautiful which exists in thought, action, or person, not our own. A man, to be greatly good, must imagine intensely and comprehensively; he must put himself in the place of another and of many others; the pains and pleasures of his species must become his own."[7] When Simon Bale enters Henry's life and tests the limits of Henry's "love," Henry, as Gardner's moral artist, is able to imagine exactly how lonely and estranged from the world Bale must feel.

---

6. *Ibid.,* 83.
7. Donald H. Reiman and Sharon B. Powers (eds.), *Shelley's Poetry and Prose* (New York, 1977), 487–88.

Bale, the religious fanatic whose wife dies in a house fire, is another of Gardner's characters from whom the protagonist learns about those darker sides of life he has ignored or has not fully understood. Bale is no passing trucker to whom Henry can give advice and sympathy and let move on into the night. He is a man whose dogmatism has removed him from humanity: "Simon Bale had no friends. He was not only an idealist but an ascetic as well . . . and the death of his wife . . . meant the end of all ordinary contact with humanity—or would have except for Henry Soames" (150). The world for Bale is only a simple series of biblical lessons, and when he is not plying his religious literature, he lacks any purpose for existence. Bale's very conversation consists only of mumbled religious platitudes that may or may not fit the topic of discussion. As Gardner makes clear, Bale's "way of seeing, above all . . . made his mission hopeless" (149).

All of the community thinks Bale is evil, and Gardner reinforces this impression by entitling Bale's section of *Nickel Mountain* "The Devil." Within Gardner's sympathetic imagination, however, Bale is never allowed to lose his humanity or become only an allegorical figure. Bale grieves over the loss of his wife and his house. He tries to thank Henry for taking him into the new home that Callie and Henry share next to the Stop-Off, and Jimmy becomes enamoured of Bale, even though Bale causes the child to have nightmares about the Devil. What is "evil" in Bale is his self-righteous attitude, his fanaticism, for he spreads only guilt instead of love.

Henry Soames is the only person on Nickel Mountain who understands Bale's narrow vision of the world. The insight comes to Henry one day as he stands, with Bale sitting nearby, gazing at the world outside his window: "It was as if one had slipped back into the comfortable world pictured in old engravings," yet "the trees and hills were like something alive, not threatening, exactly, because Henry had known them all his life, but not friendly, either: hostile, but not in any hurry, conscious that time was on their side: they would bury him, for all his size and for all his undeniable harmlessness. . . . In his present mood, watching sunset come on, he felt at one with the blue-treed mountains, and at one, equally, with the man in the dimness behind him" (152–53). Henry's transcendence, his union with the natural world in the old-fashioned Romantic sense, allows him to share the limited vision of Simon Bale: "Perhaps it was the way the light slanted in, or the way the long silver truck rolled past and went out of his hearing: Something came to him. He knew as if by inspiration how it was that a man like Bale saw the world. For an instant he too saw it: dark trees, a luminous sky, three swallows flying all portentous" (153).

In sharing Bale's view of the world, in "going out of his own nature," Henry moves a little closer to the wholeness he is seeking. Because of this insight, Henry does what he *feels* is right and over the objection of Callie and his friends allows Bale to remain in his house. Only an accident, an element of chance, causes Henry to feel responsible for Bale's death and in turn to doubt all of his good intentions. Bale's life and death seem to be a warning from Gardner that even though we may be able to sympathize with the dogmatic artist, he is a dangerous figure whose lingering effects may prove more horrible than we can imagine.

A counterpoint to Bale is Henry's long-time friend George Loomis. Although George finds Bale's religious dogmatism repulsive and is irritated at Henry's sympathy for the man, George is as locked into a limited view of the world as Bale. George's life is controlled not by his feelings or by religious convictions but by a series of absolutes from external sources. The more control he tries to exercise over his life, the more change inevitably slips in to wrest away the absolutes he has established. Although he is proud of his roots in the Catskills, his life has been shaped by the intrusive values of the modern world, particularly those portrayed on television and in movies. As a young boy, he "had driven his motorcycle around on the mountain roads in the vague hope that something new might happen, that the world might stand suddenly transfigured, transformed to a movie—a gangster picture, a love picture, anything but the tedious ruin it was" (221). When he does finally venture into the world beyond the Catskills, he is wounded in the Korean War and disillusioned by a young Japanese prostitute with whom he falls in love. Since his return home, he has lived isolated and alone on Crow Mountain where he watches television in his old house, which he keeps "dark as a tomb" (50). When Henry suggests that George might be a more suitable husband for young Callie Wells, George's reply only affirms his retreat into a world of illusion and his unwillingness to reenter life: " 'I seen on television how they act when they love you' " (54). George's disillusionment with life is reinforced by the "schlock art" of television, and his remarkable streak of bad luck only confirms the feeling that his fate is determined. His most recent accident, the loss of his right arm in a corn binder, increases the cloud of doom under which he lives: "He sometimes believed he had known all his life that he'd end up maimed, a brace on one boot, no arm in one sleeve, and no doubt worse yet to come" (222).

Gardner undercuts George's fatalism, however, by having him try to convince Henry that Simon Bale's death was not Henry's fault. " 'Simon Bale was the same as one of them Koreans, not civilized,' " George says. " 'You took him in out of the cold when his house burned and he scared your kid with his talk about the devil and you yelled at him, and out of his own stupidity he fell down the fucking stairs. You ought to have buried him like a cat and forgot it!' " (224). George appears to recognize that chance or accident can often play a significant role in life, but he is unable to accept this knowledge in his own life and cannot possibly convince Henry of something he does not believe himself. His callousness and rigidity isolate him from his fellow human beings and protect him from the harshness, dullness, and lack of purpose in the world. At the same time, his love for the mountains and for Henry, Callie, and Jimmy reveals a sensitive and compassionate nature.

Like James Page of *October Light*, George Loomis is a farmer, the descendent of generations of farmers, who has inherited the land his family has lived on since before the Revolutionary War. A fierce independence and self-sufficiency coupled with negative experiences, both real and imagined, in the outside world have driven George to the past. Like Peter Mickelsson, George Loomis retreats into the past but ironically takes with him certain values from the modern world he so despises. Since for George, as for Mickelsson, the world of the present is "shit," he clings desperately to an old house and the artifacts it holds: "With balustered porches, round-arched windows, lightning rods, cupolas, and facing the road a Victorian tower like a square, old-fashioned silo" (128), the house is filled with "things that had been in the family for two hundred years" (129). " 'Sometimes I go in and touch them,' " George tells a neighbor. "It was the richest pleasure in his life, just picking them up, knowing they were his" (130). George chooses to remain frozen in time and to suppress the feelings churning inside of him. He refuses to give in to the physical disabilities chipping away at the foundation of his self-sufficiency. As the farm chores overwhelm him and nature begins to reclaim the land he once cultivated, George merely broods on how things used to be: "Plowing had been a pleasure once—the smell of the new-turned sillion, the blue-black sheen of the cut earth rolling off straight as an arrow, dark un-

der the pines at the top of the hill, the gingerwater jug showing dull silver in the burdocks under the trees, the plowed ground richer and
warmer where the sunlight struck. He'd be conscious of both the past
and the future—riding sidesaddle on the tractor seat, one hand on the
steering wheel, the other on the plow. . . . But now it was changed.
. . . (A different life)" (132–33). George shares with Henry Soames a
strong imagination and powerful feelings for the land—essential characteristics of the moral artists in Gardner's novels—yet George has
lost the adaptability that Henry displays and has chosen to cling to a
past that no longer exists rather than embrace the changing nature of
the world and his own mutability.

Although George thinks Simon Bale is "uncivilized" and Bale believes
George is "evil," both men teach Henry Soames a similar lesson. Their
pride in their particular visions of the world and their self-righteousness
deny them the ability to love completely. Rather than participating actively in the celebration of life, they remain statically adherent to their
system of absolutes. Unlike Bale and George, Henry does not believe
in the absolutes of good and evil: " 'I don't believe there is such a thing
as pure meanness . . . or pure anything else' " (148). As Gardner's
"true artist," Henry is open to all sorts of ideas and becomes more flexible in the face of the changing circumstances of life. When Bale and
George begin arguing over religion during a busy hour at the Stop-
Off, Henry is eager to join in, not to take sides but because "there
were things that weren't getting said" (192). Henry's groping toward
truth, his willingness to explore all avenues of an issue, testing and
evaluating as he goes, represents the process of movement toward a
moral vision in Gardner's novel. "Art," Gardner has said, "is as original and important as it is precisely because it does *not* start out with
clear knowledge of what it means to say."[8] If for "art" we substitute
the names of Gardner's protagonists who achieve reintegration—who
make life art—then Gardner's statement aptly describes the process of
discovery in their lives as well as Gardner's own method of discovery
in his novels.

In contrast, Simon Bale and George Loomis represent those artists
who "put all [their] money on some easily achieved or faked structure,
some melodramatic opposition of good and bad which can by nature
handle only trite ideas."[9] Henry Soames is more at home wading into

8. Gardner, *On Moral Fiction*, 13.
9. *Ibid.*, 52.

life itself: "He would sink down into that bustle the way he would sink down into warm river water, and he would be sorry for people who weren't caught up, as he was, in the buzzing, blooming confusion" (193). By repeating William James's phrase, which he also uses in *The Resurrection*, Gardner further reveals Henry's increasing acceptance of the totality of life and moves him closer to a certain union with the world.

Although some critics have suggested that Gardner's protagonists, especially the sentimental Henry Soames, are "too good," Gardner is careful to note Henry's fallibility. Henry relies on his intuition to act, but he always possesses doubt, fear, and guilt over the moral choices he must make: to marry Callie or not, to pay for Simon's wife's funeral or not, to take Simon in or not. The greatest decision he faces results from his feelings of responsibility for Simon Bale's death — should he forgive himself or not for causing Bale's fall down the stairs? The question leads Henry to an impasse and nearly to his own death. An answer is provided only under the influence of that "buzzing, blooming confusion" that Gardner re-creates with the final gathering of family and friends at the Stop-Off.

The occasion for the gathering is the Indian Nick Blue's prediction of rain after the long, hot, sweltering drought of the summer has upset the normal routine of the farming community. Gardner uses the drought to emphasize the stifling paralysis of Henry's guilt. By associating the drought with Henry's inability to act, Gardner slows the movement of the novel and creates a sense of impending doom as Henry nearly eats himself to death. On the night Nick Blue has predicted rain, the community gathers at the Stop-Off to share with one another the joy of the moment when the first drops will begin to fall. Soon everyone realizes that rain is not coming, and Henry, despite his inner turmoil, tries to ease the growing mood of despair by refusing to accept his friends' money for the food and drink they have consumed. Henry's crazy insistence that they sing "Happy Birthday" to him seems to unite them in a small cluster of defiance against the apparently indifferent forces of nature: "And all at once, probably out of pure shock at first, they were doing it, cold sober as they were. And then a vast and meaningless grief replaced the shock. Tears streamed down Lou Millet's face, and he was choked up so badly he couldn't bring out more than every fourth word. In the beginning there were only three voices — Henry's, Old Man Judkins', Jim Millet's — then more. . . . They were singing it through again" (259–60). This small catharsis is welcomed by those who experience it, and it allows them to carry on, assured that they are not alone in the world.

After everyone but George Loomis leaves, a moment of human contact occurs that almost releases George and does release Henry from the guilt and doubt they share. George has covered up the evidence, but like Henry he has been responsible for an innocent person's death. Earlier in the novel, Gardner introduces the strange and gypsy-like Goat Lady, an old woman trying to find her "lost son." She wanders among the towns of western New York, inquiring about her son and selling goat cheese and milk. "Otherwise known as 'Mother,' " she depends upon charity for survival, and her repugnant yet innocent nature tests even Henry's compassion. She leaves the Catskills as mysteriously as she arrived, and later we learn that George Loomis has accidentally run over her with his truck and explained away her disappearance. George soon realizes that it is not so easy as he thought to "bury [someone] like a cat and forget it," no matter how far removed from normalcy the person appears to be. Thus when George tells Callie and Henry, " 'I'm beginning to believe in the Goat Lady' " (260), he is on the verge of admitting his own human frailty, his own feelings of "guilt, shame, embarrassment." The Goat Lady becomes a scapegoat, sacrificed so George may learn that accident, or chance, plays a larger part in our lives than he would like to believe. Although George does not benefit from the old woman's death, he does come close to admitting his guilt to Henry and Callie and so indirectly "saves" his friend. Henry and Callie understand that "he could tell them and be free," but George, true to his character, cannot allow the facade of the life he has built to crumble. In pitying and forgiving George for his inability to confess, Henry accepts Simon Bale's death for what it was — mere accident. "Henry looked at him. . . . George Loomis no more free than a river or a wind, and, as if unaware that he was doing it, Henry broke the cookie in his hand and let the pieces fall. . . . George had saved them after all" (261).

As a failed artist, George unknowingly sacrifices so that Henry and Callie may continue their life's journey together. George's sacrifice is through example — he has cut himself off from the community, and when given the chance to confess his "sin" and ask for forgiveness, he cannot bring himself to do it. This combination of pride and accident has condemned George to a life alone. By George's sacrifice, the past is banished, perhaps to reside forever with him on Crow Mountain. "The room was suddenly filled with ghosts" (261), ghosts that vanish as George leaves. Gardner follows the cleansing act — this great purging of the guilt and sorrow of the past—with the rain that has been so long awaited: "Sometime during the night, while they all slept . . . thunder cracked, shaking the mountains, and it rained" (262).

In the final chapter of *Nickel Mountain*, Gardner sums up the way in which Henry Soames's life has been changed. He is still a giant fat man on the verge of succumbing to a heart ailment, but he has accepted himself and his life in the community: "With the passing of time he became in reality what he was, his vision not something apart from the world but the world itself transmuted" (301). Like James Chandler, who realizes that one must celebrate not celebration but the world itself, Henry accepts the inevitability of change—the good *and* the bad of it. Like Tolstoy, he gives up fighting the flux of life and submits to it, "freely choosing what he couldn't prevent, he'd felt a sudden joy . . . as if he'd finally shoved in the clutch on the way down a long straight hill" (300). Henry sees nothing to be gained in denying change and everything to be gained by accepting it. Even the Stop-Off is gradually transformed into a full-fledged restaurant called The Maples. Again and again Gardner emphasizes Henry's acceptance of the total process of life: "He felt like a man who'd been born again" (301); "He'd grown mystical" (301); "So it was that Henry Soames had discovered the holiness of things (his father's phrase), the idea of magical change" (302). Henry reaches the equivalent of a moral artist's aesthetic wholeness.

Gardner ends *Nickel Mountain* with a parable of love connecting Henry Soames not only to the people in his community and his family but also to the world at large. In the local cemetery, Henry meets an old man and woman, strangers who are having their son's body exhumed to be moved to a new place between their own gravesites. The old woman is very religious: " 'I believe in the resurrected Lord' " (307); but the old man is a realist: " 'He's dead and rotten,' " he says of his son (306). Although their views of life, and death, are obviously different, the two old people share a bond with their son and with each other. The love that once united them still exists, if in nothing more than this final gesture for their dead son. Henry is able to grasp the significance of their actions: " 'Love—' Henry began at last, philosophically, but he couldn't think how to finish" (309). Henry Soames lacks the fluent command of language possessed by Gardner's philosophical protagonists, but Gardner's message in *Nickel Mountain* is as clear as in the academic novels—human beings are part of nature and must be able to accept completely the process of change, including the inevitable death and decay of all things. But human beings are also unique in their ability to form bonds of emotion and of the spirit with one another, and this is a power that should be affirmed in art, as it is in life.

October Light

In *October Light*, Gardner's use of the natural world to represent the potential each human being possesses, but usually never achieves, is greater than in any of his other novels. The Catskills in *Nickel Mountain* serve to remind Henry Soames that there is more to life than the narrow, angry, disillusioned view he has of his situation as the overweight owner of a run-down truck stop, and in *The Resurrection* James Chandler's retreat to his boyhood town of Batavia, New York, brings him to understand "the great Romantic flight to Nature . . . , the soul's sublime acceptance of lawless, proliferating substance: things and their motions."[10] This "listening to nature," as Gardner calls it, is a necessary part of the evolution toward reintegration that his protagonists undergo. The natural world is seen to contain the necessary truth from which each individual can learn to incorporate all aspects of his existence into a unified whole. Gardner's use of nature as a "moral center" is perhaps most emphatically and movingly depicted through his exploration of American values past and present in *October Light*.

Inspired by the nation's approaching bicentennial as he wrote *October Light*, Gardner uses the old Vermont farmer James Page to embody the values upon which America was founded. Gardner began the novel, he says, "with the opinion that traditional New England values are the values we should live by: good workmanship, independence, unswerving honesty, and so on—and one tests those opinions in lifelike situations, puts them under every kind of pressure one can think of, always being fair to the other side, and what one slowly discovers, resisting all the way, is that one's original opinion was oversimple. This is not to say that no opinion stands up, only to say that a simulation of real experience is morally educational."[11]

The nature of the conflict in *October Light* is clearly established before the novel itself actually begins, when James Page, age seventy-

10. Gardner, *The Resurrection*, 166–67.
11. Gardner, *On Moral Fiction*, 114.

two, blows his eighty-year-old sister Sally's television "all to hell" with his shotgun. For James, television represents all of the decay, corruption, and immorality of modern American life: "He'd taken the twelve gauge shotgun to it, three weeks ago now, for its endless, simpering advertising and, worse yet, its monstrously obscene games of greed, the filth of hell made visible in the world: screaming women, ravenous for refrigerators, automobiles, mink coats, ostrich-feather hats; leering glittering-toothed monsters of ceremonies — for all their pretty smiles, they were vipers upon the earth, those panderers to lust, and their programs were blasphemy and high treason."[12] James's sister, Sally Page Abbott, however, believes in " 'changing with the times' " and supports nuclear power plants, mass production, agribusiness, and the Equal Rights Amendment. "But he had, like any man, his limit, and the limit was TV" (4). The most recent argument with his sister causes James, armed with a stick of firewood, to chase Sally upstairs where he locks her in her room. For Sally, this humiliation is the "last straw," and she refuses to come out even when her niece and all of her friends beg her to make up with James. Thus this funny and poignant novel begins as a conflict between American past and American present, yet as the battle of wills between James and Sally progresses, we begin to see that the conflict is also between traditional and contemporary literary values. In its movement toward an eventual compromise and reconciliation between James and Sally, the novel suggests which values of past and present should be preserved and passed on to future generations. Such is the process of Gardner's creative methods and the development of what he calls moral fiction.

In keeping with the original premise of the novel — the testing of New England, and, in fact, of traditional American values — Gardner develops James Page as a man obsessed with the idealism and self-reliant attitudes of the Founding Fathers: " 'there was things they believed in, a sma' bit, ennaway: a vision, you might say, as in the Bible. It was *that* they lied for and fought for and, some of 'em, croaked for' " (9). James is proud that he is of old Vermont stock, and he is especially proud that he was born on the Fourth of July. Although he is a farmer descended from generations of farmers, he is not an ignorant man.

---

12. John Gardner, *October Light* (New York, 1976), 3–4. Further references to this edition will be made in the text.

His avid interest in the history of New England and of the American Revolution occupies his mind "for the length of the whole Vermont winter," when he "did practically nothing but sit pondering books . . . or reading his newspapers" (7).

James Page, the oldest of Gardner's protagonists, faces death stoically yet is inwardly afraid. He has renounced the world except for his small plot of Vermont earth, and he stands stubbornly by the absolutes he has cultivated in a lifetime of self-sufficiency. He is caught up in a web of guilt of his own making but cannot forgive himself and others for the past transgressions that caused the guilt. And he has lost the ability to love. Only through the shock of being responsible for the near-deaths of his daughter and a close friend does James begin to realize what a limited vision of the world he has created.

James's small plot of isolated land, upon which modern values are slowly making inroads, is the ever-present backdrop for the action of the novel and for James's own journey toward reintegration. The changing seasons of Vermont circumscribe his world, but he is locked as solidly into his dark vision of that world as the approaching New England winter will grip the land. For James, "all life — man, animal, bird, or flower — is a brief and hopeless struggle against the pull of the earth" (11). There is no middle ground in life: "Everything decent, James Page believed, supported the struggle upward, gave strength to the battle against gravity. And all things foul gave support not to gravity . . . but to the illusion of freedom and ascent" (12). There is no escape from the "dark and dangerous" world, and James understands "the importance of admitting it, confronting it head on, with the eyes locked open and spectacles in place" (11). He is "violently repelled by all that senselessly prettified life and, in his own dark view, belied it" (13). His mistake is that he has allowed these fixed values to isolate him from the rest of humanity. Although the sources of their discontent and their value systems are different, James and the doomed George Loomis of *Nickel Mountain* are similarly isolated by tradition. Like George's Victorian farmhouse on Crow Mountain, James's house, sitting alone on Prospect Mountain, is a fitting symbol of his self-imposed isolation. In struggling to maintain his fierce self-reliance, he has suppressed his need for the kind of human interaction that makes life more than mere "foolishness, a witless bear exploring, poking through woods" (14).

The season of the year in the novel is the "locking time" of October:

" 'There the seasons stopped awhile. Autumn was gone. Winter was not' " (121). It is the time of year when James Page and other native Vermonters "felt a subdued excitement, a new aliveness that was more, in fact, than the seasonal change in their chemistry" (120). Yet the "locking time" is also a metaphor for James's condition. James and Sally are "locked" in a battle of wills, James "locks" Sally in her room, James develops constipation and his bowels are "locked" against relief. The October light of the "locking time" is also a reminder of the nearness of the end of life for James Page. As nature shuts down operations and prepares for winter, there is a sense of ominousness as well as of hope in the air. This period, when time is stalled, is the final chance for reconciliation and celebration before darkness and death.

After relatives and friends learn of the violent confrontation between Sally and James, they attempt to intervene, as they have apparently done in past squabbles. Sally's rebellion, however, suggests a more threatening crisis than previous conflicts have produced, and one of the oldest friends of the family, Estelle Parks, soon becomes the catalyst for events leading to the reconciliation between James and Sally. A spinster and former neighbor of Sally's when Sally was married to Horace Abbott and lived in North Bennington, Estelle revives in James the affection for people close to him that he has for so long locked away. Her singularly important attribute, as we might expect of an intercessor, is her interest in the well-being of others: "She'd been quick to like people — had been gregarious all her life — but moderation was her essence" (200). She loves life, its joys and sorrows, and has no guilt feelings about her past. James and Sally, we soon see, must try to attain Estelle's balanced view of life.

With perhaps the exception of Jessica Stark in *Mickelsson's Ghosts*, Estelle Parks is the most fully developed of Gardner's saintly intercessors. She embodies not only those values necessary to move the protagonist from impasse to action but also an understanding very much like that of Gardner's protagonists who complete the journey toward wholeness. She has taught English, traveled in Europe, and lived comfortably both married and alone. Although her vision of life is more all-encompassing, Estelle Parks, like Aunt Emma Reikert in Gardner's story "The Joy of the Just," is a kind of "life artist." She seems to move with the natural flux of life, defined so well, she believes, in the lines from "Tintern Abbey":

> For I have learned
> To look on nature, not as in the hour
> Of thoughtless youth; but hearing oftentimes
> The still, sad music of humanity,
> Nor harsh nor grating, though of ample power
> To chasten and subdue. And I have felt
> A presence that disturbs me with the joy
> Of elevated thoughts; a sense sublime
> Of something far more deeply interfused,
> Whose dwelling is the light of setting suns,
> And the round ocean and the living air,
> And the blue sky, and in the mind of man:
> A motion and a spirit, that impels
> All thinking things, all objects of all thought . . . (201–202)

She possesses the intuitive notion that life has purpose and meaning and should be celebrated openly, not "locked" away in the recesses of the human heart and denied by some stubborn rationale of the mind.

When Estelle fails to talk Sally out of her room, she resorts to the only method she knows for smoothing over differences between people—she invites all of James and Sally's friends and neighbors to the Page house for an October party. The importance of this gathering is revealed when Estelle explains the odd custom of "barn-fire parties": " 'It's a fragile life. One moment we're happy and wonderfully healthy, and our children are all well, and it seems as if nothing can possibly go wrong, and the next some horrible accident has happened, and suddenly we see how things really are and we cling to each other for dear life' " (234). Like Esther Clumly in *The Sunlight Dialogues*, Estelle Parks represents the "heart" that James Page has come to neglect, and her comments about the fragility of life suggest how James, who has always been stubborn, became lost after the suicide of his son. Instead of turning to his wife and friends for support and comfort, he turned inward, isolating himself from the healing effects of the community.

James thinks of Estelle's maneuver as an invasion of privacy and a cheap trick to get Sally to come out of her room. In a perpetually cantankerous mood anyway, he is further riled by the intrusion of others upon what he considers a private conflict between Sally and himself: "He was indeed indignant at their treating his sister—however outrageous her behavior might be—as some mindless creature that could be coaxed through fire with a graham cracker" (217). No matter how much he disagrees with her, James Page respects his sister's right to have her own opinions: " 'She does a thing, she's got *reasons* for it' "

(216). As usual, James adheres to a great democratic principle in thought, but only so long as he is in control of the situation.

As more and more people enter the house, James slips out and drives down the mountain to a nearby roadhouse. He is visibly agitated by the celebration at his house, "but the thing that had mainly gotten into James Page was Estelle's smile. Old fool that he was — so he put it to himself — for an instant James had felt powerfully attracted to her, emotion rising in his chest as sharp and disturbing as it would in any schoolboy. Even now he was upset and surprised by it. . . . They were old and ugly, both of them, and the body's harboring of such emotions so long past their time was a cruel affront, a kind of mockery from heaven" (217). The breakdown of his stoic pose is the beginning of James's acceptance of his self in all of its mystifying and alarming aspects, the beginning of a journey toward wholeness.

The gathering, from which James flees, is perhaps the brightest and most moving of any created by Gardner. Many types of communal relationships and feelings are evoked, and although James Page does not take part in the celebration, he is indirectly affected by all that occurs during the coming together of friends and family in his house. Most of the characters' feelings of love for one another and for others long dead are released by the warmth and good spirits of the party. The old people look back nostalgically at the beauty of marriages broken only by the specter of death; James Page's respect for his sister and his feelings for Estelle, as well as his love for his dead son, are unveiled; and love blossoms between Estelle's great-nephew and Dr. Phelps's granddaughter. The activities of the gathering include a sermon on evolution, classical and folk music, pumpkin carvings, and the recitation of poetry by Ruth Thomas. In fact, her poem "The Cat and The Dog" reveals more about the nature of human beings than a dozen pages of descriptive prose:

> Though he purrs, the Cat's only partly here,
> Poised 'tween the hearth and the street outside.
> Half-tame, half-wild, he's a walking riddle,
> Playing both ends against the middle.
> And so Man hangs between Truths he must fear
> And the murderous animal under his hide.
> The Dog's by nature the best of his friends,
> Playing the middle against both ends. (263)

The paradox of human nature expressed in the poem is celebrated by the gathering of friends, and James Page must learn to accept this paradox in himself and in others. The gathering appears to fail at solving the conflict between Sally and James, but it is nevertheless a very successful dramatization of the total process of life that James and Sally are missing by clinging stubbornly to their individual idealistic visions.

Although Sally is attracted to the smells and sounds of the celebration below and the sermon on evolution is delivered for her benefit, she remains steadfast in her rejection of the community. Instead she retreats into the chaotic and absurd world depicted in a pulp novel she finds under the bed in her room. When *October Light* was published, most reviewers were puzzled by this novel-within-a-novel structure of the book. The inner novel Sally reads during her "strike" seems to have nothing to do with the activities of James, Sally, and the others. Yet a close look at Gardner's theory of fiction and a closer look at the novel itself reveal the neat integration of the pulp novel within the narrative of James and Sally Page. Every artist, Gardner believes, should have a sense of moral responsibility for what he or she creates. Gardner does not see such a responsibility as an imposition of a theory upon the creative process but believes "that the morality of art takes care of itself, the good, like gravity, inevitably prevailing." Gardner agrees with Tolstoy that "the highest purpose of art is to make people good by choice" and that "moral art holds up models of decent behavior; for example, characters in fiction, drama, and film whose basic goodness and struggle against confusion, error, and evil—in themselves and in others—give firm intellectual and emotional support to our own struggle." All other art, mirroring society at its worst or sermonizing about social injustice, may be "more enlightening than a thousand psycho-sociological studies" but "it is only in a marginal sense art."[13]

If art is as influential as this, Gardner says, then the poet is the legislator of mankind, as Shelley believed, and untrue or bad art contributes to the decline of civilization:

> America has moved in the direction of the moving picture. You remember the days of *On The Waterfront*—the tipped-up collar, the cigarette hanging out of the mouth. A whole generation grew up tipping up their collars and hanging cigarettes out of their mouths. That's why we've got so much cancer in middle-age people now. Movies and comic books are the main popular art forms of our moment, and they do change the way people behave. . . . Nobody's ever proved that television causes violence

or that dirty movies cause dirty behavior. But if there's the vaguest suspicion, the least danger that it might be true, then a writer ought to think about it. . . . a writer must decide how to treat [sex and violence] with a responsible concern.[14]

In *October Light*, Gardner subtly reveals how irresponsible art — the pulp novel and television — further removes Sally from reality and increases the agitation between Sally and James, leading finally to calculated violence.

Sally's initial reaction to *The Smugglers of Lost Souls' Rock* is that it is "common drugstore trash." But in blurbs on its cover, the book is highly touted by The *National Observer*, the New York *Times*, and the St. Louis *Post-Dispatch*, and Sally is drawn to the book by these titillating statements. The novel concerns Peter Wagner, who attempts suicide, fails, then descends into a maelstrom of "marijuana smuggling, fashionable gang bangs," and black revolutionists. Gardner pokes fun at the much-praised contemporary hero-as-victim, who is a failure even at committing suicide and is thus pulled along through life by the surrounding circumstances of accident and chance. The *National Observer* is quoted as calling the novel "a sick book, as sick and evil as life in America" (15). What kind of world is it, Gardner wonders, where sickness means success and evil is admirable? Already, Gardner suggests, doublespeak has invaded the realm of responsible critical and creative writing. James Page's belief that America is changing only for the worse seems correct at this point in the novel.

The longer Sally stays in her room, the more absorbed in the pulp novel she becomes. The wild escapades of Peter Wagner and the drug smugglers begin to fill her with a feeling of having missed out on life by having been born in an age of stricter moral codes: "What she wouldn't give to be growing up now, when a girl might go anywhere she pleased and do anything she liked! Those things in that novel, now, how incredible to realize that they were all, in a sense, true! Hundreds of people smoked pot every day, though she'd never gotten a chance to — she could count herself lucky she'd got a bit of sherry! — and hundreds of people had sex orgies. . . . She, Sally Abbott, had missed all that, such were the cruel mechanics of the universe, as her novel would say" (316).

14. Joe David Bellamy, *The New Fiction: Interviews with Innovative American Writers* (Urbana, Ill., 1974), 178–79.

Suddenly, with a feeling of "mysterious serenity" inspired by the novel, Sally decides to kill James by placing a crate of apples on the top of her half-opened bedroom door so that when he enters, the crate will come crashing down upon his head. Her plan, she feels, is "like a gift from heaven—not her own plan at all but something that had come out of nowhere, like the plan Peter Wagner had had about knocking off his enemies with eels, in her novel" (320-21). Sally's thoughts and actions, Gardner reveals, have been unconsciously influenced by the pulp novel. In the same way that subliminal advertising works upon its unsuspecting subject, the pulp novel has persuaded Sally that its view of the world is the true one—that violence is, in this case, entirely justifiable. These days, she rationalizes, "no body even thought twice about it" (321). Even after her niece, James's daughter Ginny, is hit on the head and almost killed by the apple crate, Sally remains in her room: "she must, she saw again, hold firm, stick tight to her principles" (372). She becomes so caught up in her novel that she confuses her family and friends with characters in the book. Like Peter Wagner, she rationalizes her actions by blaming the world and the people in it for her predicament.

While Sally feels sorry for herself and plots revenge, James Page journeys through the past on his drive down Prospect Mountain to Merton's Hideaway. As he passes the Reynolds place, the Crawford place, the Jerome place, and other farms and homes, James recalls how the former occupants once lived as a community and held certain values in union: "That had been a whole different world; gone for good" (285). Like most of Gardner's protagonists, James also despairs at the passing of the "orderly" age of heroes and is enraged at the chaotic modern age that "scoffed about 'the good old days,' made out they were nothing but misery and pain, superstition and narrow-mindedness, and all that was true and firm in them, all that was honest and neighborly and solid as a mountain was some fool illusion" (285). James makes an interesting point, for Gardner's method is to search for and test various values, past and present, in order to decide which hold up and which should be discarded. James Page knows "the good old days" were often miserable, but he also knows that they contained something worth preserving. His overreaction to the modern age, however, causes him to defend *all* values of the past, and he refuses to consider that there may be something worth embracing in the present as well. His descent from Prospect Mountain—a world of the past—into the modern world below pushes him over the edge of "anger and frustration" into calculated revenge.

As James drinks with some old friends in an isolated booth, he watches the interactions of people in the rest of the bar. He notices the lack of embarrassment and shame among a group of college professors and their wives as they argue and drink, and he follows the loose sexual flirtations between two Bennington College co-eds and two local delinquents. As James's rage increases, outside of the tavern a storm is brewing, "as if the weather had been following James Page's mood": "It was as if there was a plot against the world's survival, disaster on its way irreversible as a railroad car broken loose on a twenty-mile grade" (297). In his drunken anger, his bowels still locked tight, James is also drawn into the casual juxtaposition of sex and violence in television programming. As he stares at the television screen over the bar, he sees a show in which two policemen chase a truck, firing wildly at the driver until his "whole head had exploded" from one of the gunshots, after which the police car and the truck "went crashing into a wall of rock . . . and they both exploded." The show is interspersed with commercials showing a half-naked woman selling hair soap, a man and a horse selling cigarettes, and "a woman in a nightclub, singing to a microphone with nothing on but a stocking-like thing" (302). The "immoral" television programming, the unabashed behavior of the people in the tavern, and his friends' confession that Sally has been monitoring his telephone calls combine to unleash James's emotions. Not only is he angry with Sally but also with himself for allowing memories of his dead son and wife to come flooding back in a torrent like the storm outside: "Put off guard by wine, he'd casually wandered into a past he'd locked up tight" (303). Like many of Gardner's protagonists, James is forced back into the world by a combination of circumstances and well-meaning people. Just as the artist cannot create "true art" in total isolation, so Gardner's artist/protagonists cannot reintegrate their lives without interaction with the world. Although James embraces abstractions of the past—New England values—he has neglected the personal, and human, side of his own past.

When James leaves the bar, his intention is to confront Sally, "knocking the door down and belting her one" (309). But on the drive home he accidentally wrecks his truck, which bursts into flames. Dangling from a tree where he is thrown by the crash, he sees the burning truck as a symbol of the misery of his life, and the violence of the television program, his anger at Sally, and his guilt over his son's suicide all come together in his mind: "What he meant was that his heart had gone black as pitch. . . . he'd killed his own firstborn miserable son and would have shot himself then if it hadn't been that others were dependent on him; and these smug, rich preachers [who had come to rescue him] could stand looking down at his life on fire. . . . What he meant was: he had decided to shoot his sister" (311). When he actually appears with a shotgun to force the party guests to leave his house, he causes Ed Thomas, a close friend, to have a heart attack. Still, like Sally, he cannot give up his determined plan: "He saw in his mind's eye that picture on TV, the truck driver's head exploding when the policeman shot him, and the rage that had begun to flag was back full force" (314). The violence of television has exerted its influence upon James just as the pulp novel has led his sister to commit an act she would normally not have even considered. Art of all kinds, even bad art, Gardner suggests, can have an effect on someone whose state of mind is already in turmoil.

Despite his determination, James is worn down by the physical exertion of his journey to the roadhouse, his accident, and his confrontation with the others at his house. Soon after he wields the shotgun against his friends, he falls asleep in the bathroom, and the next morning his daughter Ginny is crushed beneath the apple crate meant for him. Ginny's nearly fatal encounter sobers James, and the additional responsibility he feels for having caused Ed Thomas' heart attack begins to affect him. Like the storm of the night before, James's anger is spent, and he seems on the verge of some sort of transformation. Gardner makes the connection between the October locking imagery and James's state of mind absolute:

> When they'd said good-bye and hung up, he sat looking out the window a while, his mind just drifting. The afternoon was as gray as the morning had been, no life but a few chickens in the yard, and he realized that this was the season he'd always forgotten, all his life, had neglected to prepare for until suddenly it was upon him, the gap between the glory of fall and the serenity of winter in Vermont, the deep soft snow of November and December, the long blue shadows of January. . . . Though it was only last night that the storm had torn them off, the leaves seemed to have lost their vitality already, their yellow dulling to a yellowish gray, the red dimming down towards orange. It was the light, perhaps, that made the leaves seem half-rotted, but if the rot hadn't really set in yet today, it would be there for sure tomorrow or the next day, and the gap of drab weather, no life but in the sky, would drag on and on, the days growing

shorter, more uncomfortable, more unhealthy, no pleasure but a few butternuts the squirrels had missed—perhaps a glimpse of a fox—until getting out of bed was the hardest of his chores, and getting back into it at night was unconditional surrender. The gap might last for weeks— gray pastures, gray skies, even the crows in the birches looking up—and then when he began to believe he would never get through it alive, there suddenly, one morning, would be the world transformed, knee deep in snow, and even if the sky was gray, the farm would be beautiful. (375)

Sally simultaneously begins to reconsider her actions. In the light of a new day the pulp novel seems silly, overwritten, and sentimental. By imagining the various types of people who might or might not need such a book to enliven the dull dreariness of their lives, she recognizes by comparison the amount of happiness she has experienced in her own life (392–96). The bizarre end of the pulp novel, in which the only promise of salvation for Peter and his gang, under attack by the Coast Guard, is a huge flying saucer descending perhaps to pick up the "lost souls," further alienates Sally from the book's excessive picture of life. She thinks of her even-tempered, morally inspiring husband, Horace Abbott, and their life together in contrast to the lives in the novel: " 'Horace,' she said wearily, 'that's the kind of thing this world's come to' " (400). In a sense, Horace is her intercessor, for he represents the values of the past worth preserving. Sally discovers that the key to survival, to understanding, is compromise. One must be able to accept the good *and* the bad of one's actions, she realizes, and to affirm the good and admit the bad without feeling guilty or angry or afraid. Sally also encounters her own "ominous stranger" when she sees the "ghost" of James's son Richard outside her window during the storm. In creating Sally Page, Gardner comes close to revealing the process of moral art in the life of a female character, but at the end of the novel, he reduces her role to that of intercessor. Sally never learns the "secret" of the ominous stranger—Richard committed suicide because he accidentally caused Horace Abbott's death—but she unknowingly and indirectly conveys this information to James.

The most poignant scene in *October Light*, and the most revealing of James's acceptance of himself and his place in the world, occurs in the subchapter "Ed's Song." With James at his hospital bedside, Ed Thomas recounts what he will miss if he dies. Ed's feelings focus on the dark and light of life, the totality of existence, the wholeness of being, represented by the seasonal changes of the Vermont countryside. In his serene, melancholy happiness at contemplating life and death, Ed displays the same mystification at the paradox of human nature as Henry Soames and Fred Clumly. " 'It's a funny world,' " Ed says, echoing both of Gardner's other protagonists. Ed tells James that he will miss the " 'steadily increasin' " blackness of winter and the January snow when there's " 'nothin alive but some deer and rabbits and snowmobiles' " (415). But most of all, Ed says, he will miss the promise of rebirth that is disguised by winter: " 'But I'll tell you what I'll miss more than ah the rest, and that's 'unlocking'. . . . That's a life, James, I'll tell you, not as if you didn't know — standin out there in the maple grove countin up your buckets like a banker, and lookin out over the hills as the whole world outside and inside unlocks' " (416–17).

When Sally finally emerges from her room and inadvertently allows James to understand that he is not directly responsible for his son's suicide, James's transformation — his acceptance of his own guilt and fear (and his son's) — seems complete: "It was as if, suddenly, he had fallen back into the world, found the magic door" (427). The guilt of twenty years falls away, and James is on the verge of achieving a kind of aesthetically whole vision, one that will allow him to salvage his remaining years with his family and friends.

If we read James Page as Gardner's moral artist, he begins the novel locked into a didactic stance, defending absolutes of the past even though many of them are obsolete or never existed. He has become static within a single vision, as if the October light were to last an entire lifetime. The gathering at his house, his descent to the modern world at Merton's Hideaway, his violent outbursts force him to face the reality of a changing world. Ed's song of the seasons reminds James Page that by focusing only on the day-to-day mechanics of keeping his farm going he has lost sight of the intimacy existing between a farmer and his land. When Ed asks him, " 'How come you're listenin to all this?' " (418) and James replies, his false teeth lost in the truck accident, " 'Becauth . . . ith true' " (418), Gardner is reemphasizing the indefinable quality of good art. Affirming as he does the universals of human experience, Ed Thomas agrees. " 'That's what I tell my Ruth,' " Ed says, " 'She's got good poems and bad poems, and she'll swear on the Bible she can't tell which is which. I explain to her only the good poems are exactly true' " (418). James understands such quality and expresses it in terms of good craftsmanship: " 'Like a good window-thash' " (418). James, as artist/protagonist, begins to realize that one must accept and appreciate changes in human nature as one accepts and appreciates changes in the seasons if one's life (art) is to contain some moral integrity.

Although James senses the worth of "Ed's Song," he does not come to a complete understanding of his life until he encounters the bear at his beehives. In the final chapter of *October Light*, appropriately labeled "(The Intruder)," James Page encounters in the flesh the bear whose image Gardner has attached to characters throughout the novel. In keeping with the novel's intense emphasis on the natural world as a model for past values that may be worth salvaging, the bear is noticed first as a metaphor for describing the uncultured yet principled attitudes of America's heroic men of action, like "the huge old foul-mouthed bear of a man Ethan Allen" (10). The bear images become associated with those values of the past, and people who cling to them, that appear to have become obsolete in the present: "All life was foolishness, a witless bear exploring, poking through woods" (14); Ed Thomas, a farmer himself, is seen by Sally as "a thoughtful bear" going about his chores; James thinks of "good workmanship" in America having been murdered, "shot dead in its sleep like a bear in the sugarhouse" (286); and Richard Page's "ghost," which Sally thinks she sees outside her window in the storm, may only be the wandering bear that later appears at James's beehives. As in Faulkner's story, the bear is an outdated representative of the wilderness that was once America and of the skills for coping with the wilderness that are apparently no longer needed. This feeling is summed up in Ruth Thomas' poem, "The Bear": " 'If someone offers you a Bear, bow low / and say 'No!' " (263). James himself is finally seen as a "lost bear hunting for the door to the underworld" (303), still suffering from the suicide of his son.

While tending his bees, James begins thinking of his long-dead wife, Ariah, and the serenity of her loving and forgiving nature. With the knowledge that she kept the secret of the reason for their son's suicide to herself, suffering for her son who had extracted the promise of secrecy from her and for her husband who was left thinking that he alone had driven Richard to his death, James, like Fred Clumly, finally comprehends the undivided and sacrificial loyalty of his wife. No longer burdened by guilt from the past, James begins at last to savor the memories of his family. Suddenly, an ominous shadow comes over him and "there was a smell of wilderness." He looks up from the hive to see an old but powerful six-hundred-pound black bear "five feet away from him, between him and the gun" (433): "The two ancient creatures stared at one another, both of them standing more or less upright" (433). James believes he is feeling what "that Britisher" must have felt when he "beheld that stone man Ethan Allen towering against the stars and gray dawn. . . . He, the Britisher, had been an ordinary man, as James Page, here among his hives, was only an ordinary man. Ethan Allen had been put upon the earth like Hercules, to show an impression of things beyond it" (433). By emphasizing his own ordinariness, James reveals his reintegration with the "community." In addition, his association of the bear with the superhero Ethan Allen suggests a confrontation with the possibilities for heroic action that have been all but lost. The bear seems to stand for the essence of life that carries over through time, those values of the past that are worth preserving, just as the animal itself, most species of which are on the verge of extinction in the wild, is worth preserving. When the bear goes to all fours and begins eating honeycombs, James reflexively grabs for his shotgun. Instead of shooting the bear, he only fires wildly into the air, frightening the animal away, for it seems to him that the bear embodies not only the heroic stature of Ethan Allen but also the decency and happiness, the eternal forgiving nature of his wife: "It had seemed to the old man that the bear had said something, had said to him distinctly, reproachfully, *Oh James, James!*" (434). His dead wife's voice seemingly emanating from the bear reminds him of the futility of his stubbornness and guilt and at the same time offers benediction. Although Estelle Parks and Sally Page act as living intercessors, only the great love that James and his wife Ariah had for one another can bring him grace.

In the process of their composition and revision, John Gardner's novels "naturally," as he would say, dramatize the essential and universal morality of life. The path to discovering this morality is the human imagination. The characters of Gardner's novels, if they are to succeed in affirming an inherent morality in life, "must imagine intensely and comprehensively . . . to put [themselves] in the place of another and of many others," just as the artist does in creating distinct individual characters. When the imagination and its corollaries sympathy, compassion, and understanding are made stagnant by contemporary life or are repressed by social values, Gardner's characters only have to look around them at the ever-changing natural world in which they live. Nature, for Gardner, reflects the human condition. By opening themselves up, by recognizing the infinite number of human attitudes and visions of life, Gardner's characters come to understand the connectedness of the world and move toward the "aesthetic whole-ness" for which they are searching. Thus through the contemplation of nature, and the wholeness it contains, James Page, like Henry Soames, is able to reach the state of broad perception in which, as Gardner says, "one is capable of embracing all experience as holy, and some experience as *more* holy."

3

Conversations with Seers
The Wreckage of Agathon and *The Sunlight Dialogues*

If you show characters struggling to know
what's right, and in the *process* of the novel you
work out their issues more and more clearly,
whether the character heroically wins or
tragically loses, then you move the
reader. —JOHN GARDNER

The Wreckage of Agathon

In *The Wreckage of Agathon* and *The Sunlight Dialogues*, John
Gardner's focus shifts from protagonists who dominate the action to
those who share it with Satanic seers, as if Gardner had decided to allow us into the mind of Simon Bale in *Nickel Mountain* rather than to
reflect his feelings through Henry Soames's limited consciousness.
With Agathon and Taggert Hodge, the Sunlight Man, Gardner gives
as much attention to the failed artist as to the artist/protagonist who
achieves some sense of reintegration and attempts to "make life art."
In these two novels, we see more clearly than in any others how keenly
Gardner feels the frustration and sadness of the artist who is unable to
negotiate his own madness and isolation and whose stubborn belief in
"art for art's sake" can lead only to failure.

Although both Agathon and Hodge have been called protagonists,
they do not represent the philosophy or behavior of Gardner's moral
artist. For Agathon and Hodge, redemption is impossible. Before the
novels begin, their lives have been firmly fixed on the paths they have
chosen, and they maintain their courses without alteration. In *The
Sunlight Dialogues*, we are given, with nearly equal weight of characterization, the stories of Taggert Hodge and Fred Clumly. Hodge is
condemned through his participation in at least three murders and by
his obsession with his own unique "art" of revenge and blessing, but

Clumly is eventually saved by Hodge's intervention in his life and by the kind of enlightenment typical of Gardner's artist/protagonists. In *The Wreckage of Agathon*, Agathon's story and character so dominate the narrative that to suggest he is *not* the moral artist figure at first seems unreasonable. Yet Agathon does not appear to experience a definite reintegration or epiphany before his death. The key to this initial puzzle is resolved, I believe, if we refer briefly to *Grendel* and to the relationship between Taggert Hodge and Fred Clumly in *The Sunlight Dialogues*.

Grendel, as critics have pointed out, represents the beast in all of us, and a common misreading of Gardner's plan in *Grendel* is to see the monster as an affirmation of beastliness and howling emotion. Stephen Singular, for instance, says "Gardner takes the reader so far inside the head and heart of the monster that he finds himself cheering for Grendel even as the beast kills and eats women and men." Singular reacts in the way Gardner wants him to, but he misses the point of Gardner's use of first-person narration. As an artist, Grendel possesses a convincing vision, like the visions of those postmoderns who play to the cynicism in all of us, but the "monstrous literature" produced by such a vision, Gardner would say, cannot survive the test of time. We sympathize with Grendel because we are restricted to his point of view and because Gardner's treatment of even his most horrific character, as well as of his other characters of somewhat questionable natures, reveals a compassion rare in character development in contemporary fiction. Grendel's physical nature (he is a monster in the sense of all that the word brings to mind) does not allow for the possibility of reintegration. From the negative example of Grendel's life, however, the reader gains insight into the power of art and human love over darkness and evil, for moral fiction is not only "fiction that gives you an idea how to live," as Gardner has pointed out, but also fiction that shows you how not to live.[1]

Taggert Hodge in *The Sunlight Dialogues* is another example of a character for whom we have sympathy but who has lost his chance for salvation. He takes on the role of teacher in his relationship with Fred Clumly and in his performance in the community. From the confrontation of opposites — Hodge's "ideal freedom" and Clumly's rather fascistic adherence to law and order — emerges a compromise, but only

---

1. Stephen Singular, "The Sound and Fury Over Fiction," *New York Times Magazine* (July 8, 1979), 38; Paul F. Ferguson, *et al.*, "John Gardner: The Art of Fiction LXXIII," *Paris Review*, XXI (Spring, 1979), 73.

Clumly, the pupil, is the recipient of its benefits, only Clumly undergoes the epiphany characteristic of Gardner's moral artists.

In *The Wreckage of Agathon*, Agathon embraces Grendel's bestial existence willingly, for as seer of Sparta he plays the role of our own century's eccentric "shaman/artist," and he has assumed the role of teacher not only for Sparta generally but, as with Hodge, for a specific pupil Demodokos, whom he calls "Peeker." With such direct parallels to Grendel and Hodge, Agathon must be read as a magnificent failure but as a "minor artist" nevertheless. Agathon's failure as a moral artist is a result of his deliberate isolation from society during the same time he attempts to provide a model by which it can judge itself. In comparing the three novels, we can only conclude that Gardner's moral artist is the Shaper in *Grendel*, Fred Clumly in *The Sunlight Dialogues*, and Peeker in *The Wreckage of Agathon*. Gardner, in fact, has said that Peeker is the hero of *The Wreckage of Agathon*, and when the apprentice seer meets with Agathon's wife Tuka, in a scene as startling and as moving as the one in which James Page participates at the end of *October Light*, we know he has been given the gifts necessary to understand himself and his life in the manner of Gardner's other moral artists.[2] The tendency to overlook Peeker is, of course, a result of his youth, his relative innocence and naïveté, and his apprenticelike narrative. My point is that *The Wreckage of Agathon* is the portrait of a failed artist, a portrait created by that artist's own words and from which Peeker may learn what the reader learns by the end of the novel. Agathon, in a sense, writes to teach us as well as Peeker, and the true "wreckage," or tragedy, is that Agathon himself cannot benefit from what he writes. Time, for him, has run out.

The Wreckage of Agathon and *The Sunlight Dialogues* are linked as well by their obvious reflections of the turbulent times, the sixties, in which Gardner wrote them. That the debates over law and order versus freedom in both novels do not slide into didacticism is testimony to Gardner's ability to create the kind of balanced narrative that he establishes as an ideal in *On Moral Fiction*. In *The Wreckage of Agathon*, neither the great though decadent democracy of Athens nor the orderly though soulless police state of Sparta is condemned or praised, for they reflect the rigid ideological stances of the United States and the Soviet Union, the uncompromising positions of the liberal intel-

---

2. Marshall L. Harvey, "Where Philosophy and Fiction Meet: An Interview with John Gardner," *Chicago Review*, XXIX (Spring, 1978), 85.

igentsia and the conservative Nixon White House in the U.S., and the seemingly irreconcilable desires for order and freedom within the human condition.[3]

Although deemed a "pastoral" novel, *The Wreckage of Agathon* downplays the natural world as an influence on people.[4] We are always aware of the classical beauty of Greece as backdrop, but Agathon does not engage nature directly and does not derive strength and insight from it. For Agathon, the natural world is not an external force but a state of mind. Like the people he "loves" and the cities he lives in, nature, he believes, is subject to his "will." At the beginning of the novel when Agathon imaginatively reverses the seasons so that he will die not in the full flowering of summer but in a world frozen in snow and ice, presided over by indifferent distant stars in a dark winter sky, he reveals both his power as an artist and his stubborn refusal to embrace the world as it is.

Agathon sees the natural world as part of a mechanistic universe, as he reveals in his account of a long-past conversation with his fellow student Konon. " 'I believe in the stars,' " Konon replies when Agathon asks him about his religious faith: " 'I believe in rivers, mountains, sheep, cattle, horses, gold, and silver. . . . It's better to believe there are no gods, be satisfied with substance. . . . Everything on earth is substance. All the rest is drunkenness and illusion. . . . You know what death is? An abandoned body . . . a broken machine. . . . And religion, that's a machine, too: a mechanical system of words and howls and lifted arms that you start up to comfort some fool and abandon as soon as he's comforted. Politics, honor, loyalty—all machines.' "[5] Agathon's later insistence on "second by second"—his phrase for defining truth (and a phrase echoed by the failed artists of Gardner's "The King's Indian")—reveals his eventual adoption of Konon's view of the world. Any attempt to impose order lasting longer than "a second" is doomed to failure, and those who cling to such illusions are fools. This dismissal of all means of imposing order, including love, is very similar to the philosophical stances of contemporary writers whom Gardner takes to task in *On Moral Fiction*, and we soon see that Konon's actions belie his words. His attempt to assassinate Solon, ruler of Athens, and his trust of Agathon with the secret

3. Cowart, *Arches and Light*, 30–31.
4. *Ibid.*, 27–32.
5. John Gardner, *The Wreckage of Agathon* (New York, 1970) 140–141. Further references to this edition will be made in the text.

of his plan reveal his cynicism and despair, but also his idealism and faith. In Agathon's betrayal of his friend, despite the double bind of his situation (he prevents Solon's death but causes Konon's execution), can be found the essential failure of his life — his inability to love or to understand the power of love.

Ironically, the closest Agathon comes to expressing the kind of deeper love that Gardner values is in a brief reflection on the landscape of Sparta:

> I have sometimes stood on a hill in summertime, looking over the miles and miles of blowing wheat and barley this fertile land produces, the deep green pastures — specked with goats and cows and sheep, studded here and there with elm and maple trees — the land parted, as if gently, by wandering streams, and split down the middle by the wide, smooth-as-a-mirror Eurotas with its fishing boats and pleasure boats and its children swimming, splashing each other and laughing. I have gazed at the peaceful old temple to Orthia rising out of the marshy borderland, its white reflection motionless in the water. . . . And sometimes at night, on a fast horse, I have ridden that countryside alone, my head down close to the horse's neck, my nostrils flaring to suck in his smell. The still night air would go rushing past my ears and the stars hung motionless, poised to strike, as if not a mile above me. I'd gallop down lanes where the smell of grapes rose from either side like fine perfume, down wide dirt roads that by day would be filled with Helot wagons piled high with cabbages or bundles of cloth, and I'd ride through villages where even the poorest were richer than most of the world. No such abundance leaps out of the earth around Athens. (207–208)

Despite this moving confession of connectedness with the natural world, Agathon's actions suggest that his love is not so much for the beauty of nature or for people as it is for the possibilities of an ideal state (another form of Gardner's ever-present pastoral Eden), an ideal that has now been ruined by Lykourgos's rule and the subjugation of the Helot natives. In coping with this failure — with existence in a less-than-perfect world — several people close to Agathon, including Lykourgos, Dorkis, and even a prison guard, have developed a life-affirming dignity. With the words "I did not simplify," Agathon also claims such dignity, but his claim has no validity. By his own account, Agathon has eschewed all universal human values in favor of ideals. He has loved ideas more than the land or its people.

In the same way that he contemplates the landscape but does not understand its varied significance, Agathon reflects on the loves of his life but never grasps the total significance of these relationships. Agathon's inability to understand creates a greater irony because the philosophical focus of the novel is on the value of love. As one might expect of a novel written during the "sexual revolution" and set in classical Greece, *The Wreckage of Agathon* reflects the open-minded, even casual, attitudes toward sexuality prevalent in both periods of time. The novel also contains John Gardner's most explicit handling of sexual relationships until *Mickelsson's Ghosts*. Yet sexual love is only one of the multiple types of love dealt with in the novel. Gardner's reliance on Greek mythology and philosophy, in keeping with his choice of setting and time, allows him to explore the multifaceted emotion that our own time has made nonspecific. The novel contains references to the forms of love (heterosexual, homosexual, parental, filial, conjugal, and fraternal love; friendship; love of country; and love of wisdom) distinguished by Greek philosophy. Careful distinctions are also made between the belief of classical mythology that love is the enemy of reason and the later view of classical philosophy that love is a power for union (composition) in opposition to strife (the power of external forces that cause decomposition). Through Agathon, Gardner develops various attitudes toward love, but eventually, it seems to me, puts Agathon in league with Schopenhauer (from whom the epigraph for the novel is taken), who condemned love in very much the way of classical mythology and the older Greek poets, and who defined art as the ultimate experience but one divorced from moral aims.

Agathon's account of his youth is a kind of self-deception, yet out of it arises the truth about his own nature. The greatest love of his life, Agathon tells us, has been divided between two women—Tuka, his wife, and Iona, wife of his closest friend in Sparta, the Helot Dorkis: "They were, both of them, goddesses in the only sense of the word I understand. They were embodiments of heavenly ideals—conflicting ideals—that my soul could not shake free of. Tuka . . . had the precision of intellect, the awesome narrowness of purpose, of a mathematician or a general. She knew, beyond any shadow of a doubt, what she wanted from life and why. . . . Iona wanted not some one thing but everything; she had a mind as wide, as devious and turbulent, as a poet's, and she went for what she desired like a swarm of blind bees in a windstorm" (55–56). Agathon uses the simple dichotomy of Tuka as "head" and Iona as "heart" to classify his lovers, but his lengthy descriptions of the two women conflict with his classification of them. Tuka emerges not as an "awesomely narrow intellect" but with the "antiphilosophical mind of a mad musician," and Iona's beauty does not represent a diffuseness of mind but disguises a militant revolutionary with one cold, single-minded aim. Either Agathon has forgotten the real reasons for his attraction to Tuka and Iona, which is not likely, or in retrospect he has chosen to "misread" his lovers because they exposed his weaknesses. Agathon's reference to the women as "goddesses" supports the latter supposition, for in the history of philosophy, goddesses of love are enemies of reason, and we know that Agathon prides himself on his powers of reason.

Having known Tuka since childhood (she is the daughter of his teacher's master, Philombrotos), Agathon remains attracted to his wife partly because of their lengthy camaraderie, partly because of his inability to penetrate the mystery of her being, and partly because of her social brilliance. As a playmate, girl friend, lover, and finally wife, Tuka complements Agathon in his divergent roles as "second-most famous poet in Athens," Athenian diplomatic representative (and spy) to Sparta, and "seer of Sparta." "I knew, I suppose, how I felt about her, but she was to me some higher form of life, as distant from me as a goddess would be from a cow" (69), Agathon says of her when they are teenagers, and he never loses this awe. Years later, at social functions in Sparta, the same sense of pride and mystery fills Agathon's description of his wife: "[Tuka] was radiant, casually elegant as a mountain temple, so conscious of her easy superiority of taste and class that she could lay them aside like a shawl" (45). Agathon finds Tuka sexually attractive as well, although she is no great beauty and his affairs with Iona and Thalia, wife of a young Athenian "black-market king," are more sexually stimulating than his marriage to Tuka.

Agathon attributes the powerful attraction he feels for Tuka to her intellectual powers, but their long friendship, her wealthy background, and her sensuality create a comfortable security for him. He is also attracted by her mysterious powers as a musician and her occasional inexplicable cruelty. When Tuka plays her harp, Agathon says, "She would play, then, as if feeling were all there were in the world, and nature had no resistance. I would open my eyes and lie motionless, listening with every nerve to the music moving through the night's deep quiet like a god out taking a walk. . . . I looked from one object to another in the room, and everything that detached itself from the general dimness stood transmuted" (62). In the use of his favorite word, *transmuted*—often connected with his protagonists' moments of epiphany—Gardner underscores the importance of Tuka's music in Agathon's life. Agathon precedes Schopenhauer in the belief that music is purer than other art forms and cannot be explained by a "theory of Ideas," for he is affected by Tuka's playing in a way he cannot put into words. Tuka herself is transformed by the music and becomes its medium, as Agathon will soon become the seer of Apollo: "as she played . . . she was inside the music, moving only as the music moved, swaying for an instant, hovering, sometimes touching the dark wood beam of the harp with her face as though the harp, too, knew the secret" (63). As he listens to Tuka's playing, Agathon experiences a moment when he is both divorced from the world and connected to all things in and of it, a moment that Joan Orrick, another of Gardner's failed artists, calls the "stillness" at the center of "true art." Like Joan and other artistic failures in Gardner's *The Art of Living*, Agathon senses the power of art, especially of music, as an entity unto itself, yet he cannot reconcile its ordering power with the chaotic world of death and decay in which he lives.

As one might also expect of any artist portrayed in Gardner's work, Tuka has a touch of blind passion, and in her case it takes the form of senseless cruelty to other human beings. Agathon says of her unpredictable nature—part tomboy, part aristocrat, part sexual goddess, part musician, part sadist—"I would stare in disbelief, shrinking back, wincing, struggling to make her fit with anything I knew of mundane reality. I could connect it with nothing I'd ever felt—or, anyway, could remember feeling" (63). The mystery of Tuka's nature has a powerful effect on Agathon, for his long relationship with her is a kind of adventure, and although he claims he loves her, his love of people, as he admits, is "second to adventure and ideas." Agathon loves only the idea of Tuka, or rather *his* idea of what Tuka may be.

Agathon's narrow vision and his awe of Tuka are further revealed if we understand that Agathon himself possesses characteristics similar to those he finds attractive in Tuka. Like Tuka, Agathon is proud of his Athenian heritage: "an Athenian, heir to the old Mykenaian and Ionian civilizations, no Spartan savage come down from the Dorian mountains." Like Tuka, Agathon is subject to the pure power of art; he is Apollo's seer. Peeker's description of Agathon in a trance much resembles Agathon's feelings upon hearing and seeing Tuka play her harp. "There's a look he gets," Peeker says, "as if his spirit has abandoned his body, leaving it old and indifferent as a mountain. He's going to make me a Seer, he says. I've believed it sometimes, but not at those times when that thing comes over him, that deadly, heatless clarity of Apollo's light" (134). And, like Tuka, Agathon is possessed, not by the feigned madness of "Agathon the seer," but by a deeper, uncontrollable rage that flashes forth unpredictably. As we discover at the end of the novel, this rage had led him to "kill" those people he "loves" best, among them Konon and his own brother. Tuka confesses to Peeker that Agathon would have "killed her, too," if she had not left him. The relationship of Tuka and Agathon is based not on love, but on the mysteries and similarities they see reflected in one another. Like artists who cling blindly to their art, isolated from the world and its community of human feeling, Tuka and Agathon cling to one another until Agathon gives up his "love" to become the "mad seer." At the end of the novel, it seems fitting that Peeker is apparently passed from Agathon to Tuka in order to continue his movement toward the knowledge required of a moral artist, for although Agathon is a failure at making life art, Tuka continues to affirm life, as her immersion in the art of music and her continuing participation in family life and society make clear. We sense that Peeker will learn not only from Agathon's mistakes but also from Tuka's "art of living."

Agathon's other goddess, Iona, radiates pure sensuality from the moment Agathon first meets her: "Her breasts were like cream, like snow-capped mountains, as perfect as sacrificial doves, and exposed to the very halo of the nipple. No naked Spartan girl could have dreamed of competing" (43). Although Iona's sensuality is a powerful force, much of Agathon's attraction to her seems to be stimulated by her Helot origins and his own effect on her: "I was, at least from a Helot point of view, a person of importance: an Athenian. . . . the personal guest of Lykourgos, living in his palace, at times his unofficial diplomatic envoy. . . . What power [Iona] must have thought she had within her grasp! . . . She would show me what culture the Helots maintained in semisecret, would ravish me with food and flowers and music and her clever husband's talk" (42). As he unconsciously acknowledges, Agathon is seduced perhaps as much by Iona's flattery of his sense of superiority as by her physical beauty.

Yet when the sexual consummation of their relationship occurs after a long period of intimate meetings and discussions (and then only after Tuka seduces Iona's husband Dorkis), Agathon experiences a type of love that he never believed existed: "I leaned on my arm beside her and, after I'd thought about it, closed my hand on her breast. The effect shook me to my roots, hurled me back into the innocence of childhood. The softness of her flesh was like a sudden bursting of wells in a desert, like sympathy, kindness, and understanding I'd forgotten I deserved. It was as if all I'd been when I was good, when I was young, had lain in moldering disuse until that instant. All the tension I'd hardly known I felt came unwound. I was clean" (101). Although Agathon begins the relationship by attempting to seduce Iona with his philosophizing, his musings become more and more confessional under the spell of Iona's "innocent" sexuality. Iona becomes a kind of Beatrice for Agathon, to whom he must confess his innermost feelings, yet he wants not to share his life with her but to absorb her life into his own: "I was horrified anew at the violence of my feeling for her. It shook my world like the wrath of Poseidon and left nothing familiar, nothing even recognizable. . . . My whole life was meaningless. I was free. Also caught. It wasn't her body I wanted, or not just that. I wanted *her*" (102). With Iona, Agathon comes closer to succumbing to the passion of love, its jealousies and doubts, pleasures and comforts, than with any other person. She embodies those pastoral pleasures of fruitfulness and innocence that release Agathon's feelings, but he fails to see that Iona's "love" is not reciprocal and her attractive and often inspirational presence disguises a deadly earnestness of design.

From the very beginning of the relationship, Iona desires Agathon not for love or for sex but for revolution. With his access to Lykourgos and his passion for rhetoric, Agathon, in Iona's view, would make a brilliant spy and an excellent recruiter for the Helot underground. But Iona's single-mindedness is both a virtue and a flaw. At the end of the novel, an old and unattractive Iona, withered by her obsession with a single idea and still determined that Agathon can aid the revolution, plots his escape from prison: " 'We're going to make you well; as soon as you're well you'll help us. We need your mind, your knowledge of them, your way of swaying people' " (214-15). Iona, despite her intercessorlike effect on Agathon, is hardly a figure of perfect virtue. Her idealism and sexuality touch Agathon's innermost feelings and desires, yet her obsession with the overthrow of Sparta eventually leads to the death of her husband Dorkis, the loss of her standing in the community, and the end of her relationship with Agathon. Love, Agathon concludes from his experience with Iona, merely distorts reason. Consequently, neither Agathon nor Iona ever realizes that there are human values more important and more lasting than an ideal or an abstract freedom.

Unlike Tuka and Iona, Thalia appeals only to Agathon's sexual desires. By allowing Agathon a third lover, Gardner further distinguishes the intensity of Agathon's relationships with Tuka and Iona from the commonplace of his sexual affairs with other women. His love for Tuka and Iona stems from needs other than the physical, whereas his sexual use of Thalia is only a temporary escape from problems and pressures: "Thalia never possessed me, body and soul. For her, as for them, I felt tenderness, respect, admiration. Like theirs, her unexpected appearance in a room gave my heart a sudden leap of pleasure and, needless to say, desire. But she was never inside me like an incubus bent on my destruction. It was like the difference between a reflection in a clean pool and a reflection seized by a water spirit as a mask for her deadly courtship. What it was that made the difference I don't know" (129–30). Agathon uses Thalia only to prove his manliness and to satisfy doubts that Tuka and Iona raise about his physical and moral superiority.

Like John Horne in *The Resurrection*, Thalia's husband Hamrah reveals the narrow-mindedness toward which Agathon is moving, and like James Chandler, Agathon dismisses him. At one point in their friendship, Hamrah tells Agathon, " 'People do two things. . . . They *think* and they *feel*. When what people think goes against what they feel, feeling should be slapped unconscious. That's humanness' " (131–32). Agathon's eventual acceptance of just such a view is supported by his statement that his affair with Thalia occurs when "something had snapped, in all of us; whatever it was that had held things together—some illusion upon which we'd agreed—had lost its power" (131). This loss of an "illusion upon which we'd all agreed" is the beginning of Agathon's shift from a pursuit of love and the values inherent in community to a retreat into isolation and a complete reliance upon reason. Whereas Gardner's artist/protagonist rejects society only to seek it out again as part of a conscious or unconscious attempt at reintegration, Agathon never returns to the "illusions" of order that make life worth living. For Agathon, nothing has value, "nothingness" is all there is, and art cannot ever change the reality of human rottenness: "The lover writes because the emotion that charges every line . . . will give him no rest until he's set it down. . . . Art is more dignified than life, and, to just that degree, more deathlike. . . . The lover remains, for all his fine words, a hungry, fallible, dissatisfied child, badly in need of a fallible, all-forgiving mother; and the lady remains, for all her borrowed dignity and green incandescence, a girl child groping in alarm through a forest, in desperate search for a father. The light of Apollo . . . gives comfort, resignation, perhaps even peace, but not hope" (138–39). Unable to look within himself and rediscover those eternal verities out of which all hope (and love) springs, Agathon is lost to the world and becomes the "mad" seer of Sparta whose only valuable role is as teacher of Peeker.

If Agathon were more receptive to the rituals and verities in life, he could learn to recapture the innocence and genuine feeling of his youth by emulating Iona's husband Dorkis. Dorkis is both an intercessor for Agathon and the ominous stranger of the novel, but Agathon appears unable to grasp the significance of either role. For anyone familiar with Gardner's work, there is no doubt that Dorkis speaks for Gardner. When Dorkis and Agathon converse, usually on a philosophical level, Dorkis always presents a case not for the revolution (in which he secretly has a major role) but for the "buzzing blooming confusion" of life itself. In reaction to Agathon's tendency to rationalize, Dorkis replies, " 'You get in the habit of thinking you do things for certain reasons, but you don't. All you can do is act, somehow, and pray' " (152). Retreat or isolation or passivity is not Dorkis' way. Significantly, Dorkis echoes Henry Soames when he argues, " 'There's a sense in which nothing is evil. . . . To certain people, everything that happens in the world is holy' " (153). Dorkis is the only character in *The Wreckage of Agathon* (except for Peeker, who represents only possibilities) who possesses the vision of Gardner's moral artist.

Ironically — or perhaps inevitably — Dorkis turns out to be the "Snake," a legendary figure in the Helot rebellion, yet his participation in the revolution, as I have suggested, is motivated more by love for his country (the natural world itself, not the political state) and love for Iona than for political ideals. His sacrifice is not for the greater good of the revolution but for Agathon, a fellow human being for whom he feels compassion and love. Agathon learns from Dorkis' death but is unable to apply what he learns to his own life:

> . . . the guards brought Dorkis close to the desk. He looked down at me and faintly smiled. They'd broken his teeth and smashed the powerful cheek muscles, but they hadn't changed him, hadn't even touched him. The wounds were mere facticity.
> "Agathon," he said, moving his mouth with difficulty. "Bless you."
> . . . I was impressed; in fact, awed. Shackled, beaten, Dorkis seemed more powerful than all of them. It seemed to me for an instant that he had learned something of unspeakable importance, but the next instant I doubted that — it was my silly philosopher's prejudice, that power comes from knowledge. It struck me . . . that Something had learned Dorkis. It was as if one of his gods had gotten inside him, had taken over. (196)

Just as Agathon senses the power inherent in Tuka's artistic nature, he also feels "Something" of Dorkis' sacrificial dignity, yet he cannot reconcile either with his "philosopher's prejudice." At Dorkis' execution, Agathon notes, "He was separate—totally, absolutely—separate from everything around him. It was as if he had at last, without thinking about it, accepted something, and the choice had transmuted him. . . . And suddenly I knew. He had accepted evil. Not any specific evil, such as hatred, or suffering, or death, but evil as a necessary principle of the world—time as a perpetual perishing, space as creation and wreckage" (197–98). Agathon's intuition is correct, but he is unable to affirm it in his own life. For Gardner, evil and death are only parts of a whole, but for Agathon, entropy is all. Agathon's powers as seer only limit rather than expand his vision. Somewhat like the dragon in *Grendel*, Agathon can see the beginning and the end of all things, and he is led by such knowledge to believe that the moments in between—life itself—are meaningless. His philosophy of "second by second" is not *carpe diem* but nihilism; he insists on gazing into the abyss until it swallows him. Thus Agathon's acceptance of his own death at the end of the novel is more resignation than transmutation.

Peeker's role in Agathon's final days takes on more significance as the novel progresses. At the beginning of the novel, Peeker does not share Agathon's vision of a "wintry world" because for him the world is still in summer. He "sees" as one who is young, inexperienced, and unsure of his role. The thought of death in midsummer is very real and very frightening. Agathon's obsession with the past and his lack of concern with his impending doom are incomprehensible to Peeker, for if Peeker has the possibility of becoming Gardner's moral artist, he is yet an apprentice. Although Peeker's comments on the action and on what Agathon tells him and writes down about his life are tempered by inexperience and lack of understanding, his love for his teacher is readily apparent, and Peeker soon begins to supply information about Agathon's life that the famous seer omits, perhaps purposely, from his narrative. For instance, Dorkis' capture comes about when he "blows his cover" to save Agathon from being stoned to death by the Helots. As related by Peeker, this story of Agathon's "lost scrolls" is significant in several ways and involves the only large gathering in this novel.

Parties, recitals, reunions, funerals, or weddings often serve as climactic scenes in Gardner's novels, during which life is "celebrated and mourned" and out of which arise the protagonists' reintegrations, but the only gathering in *The Wreckage of Agathon* in which we see Agathon as a participant rather than as a commentator or observer is when the Spartans set a tomb on fire to drive out Helot rebels hidden there and inadvertently burn Agathon's scrolls. In Peeker's recounting of the event, Agathon gains possession of many precious scrolls of "dead knowledge" and hides them in a tomb in Sparta where he can retreat to study them whenever he pleases. In response to the burning of the hall of ephors by Helot rebels, the Spartan Civic Guard begins an intensive search of the city for those responsible. Still under the power of Iona, Agathon tells the rebels of his secret hiding place, and all but the leaders—Iona, Dorkis, and a few others—hide in the tomb. Tipped off to the hiding place, the Spartans burn it, incinerating all inside. The suggestiveness of Gardner's prose—"No one knows for sure what happened then. Some Spartan saw them going in, or some informer revealed their hiding place" (165)—points again to Agathon as an informer, although such a betrayal, for the resulting furor it might bring among Helots, would not be beneath Iona either.

The importance of the episode is that Agathon is traumatized by the burning of his scrolls. A certain pity for him is elicited by Gardner's careful description of his frantic attempts to salvage something from the blackened remains that crumble at his touch, yet Agathon is so obsessed with his scrolls that he is "indifferent to [the] lives and sorrows" of the Helots who are pulling their dead from the smoking tomb. The horror of his actions is soon recognized, and the Helots begin to stone him. Only Dorkis' intervention saves his life, and just barely, for Agathon receives a severe concussion and survives only through Dorkis' ministrations. Agathon's self-imposed isolation from the community is graphically realized, and his love of ideas to the exclusion of humanity is fully revealed. Nevertheless, he gains the reader's sympathy, not because of the loss of his scrolls but because of the loss of connection to the rest of society. Later, after Dorkis has been apprehended and tortured, Agathon is allowed to meet with him. Dorkis offers a kind of benediction and sadly tells Agathon, " 'You care more for knowledge than for people,' " to which Agathon starts to protest. " 'Don't fret,' " Dorkis tells him, " 'I haven't said I don't love you for it' " (167). Clearly, with this compassionate condemnation, Agathon is lost.

Dorkis' dignity arises from his deep affection for Agathon and from his Christ-like forgiveness of the Spartan government that tortures and executes him. Agathon claims a similar dignity but never achieves it, even with his own death from the plague. He mourns his inability to love anything other than "adventure and ideas," but he also realizes he can do nothing to change his own nature. As an artist, he is devoted to "his art" to the exclusion of all else, and at the same time his vision, like that of the postmodern writers whom Gardner condemns, is fixed on the "abyss": "Everything I said, everything I ever did was somebody else's, not mine. An empty ritual, nothingness" (149). Agathon's inability to transcend such an image of himself and the world, in spite of his seerlike powers, costs him his chance for redemption. Peeker is correct when he deduces from his teacher's "tales of love" that "Agathon, the great lover, hates people" (164).

As the novel unfolds, Agathon already possesses the knowledge he delivers to us via his journal, which Peeker usually reads before the ephors take each stack of writing away. Yet Agathon cannot act on what he has learned. The sense that Peeker is the true artist of the novel is reinforced by his relation of very important pieces of information about Agathon's life. In effect, he absorbs the artist Agathon's creation and then adds to it. Peeker also undergoes the usual epiphany of Gardner's moral artists when he meets Tuka at the end of the novel, but his journey toward anything like "aesthetic wholeness" has only begun, for, as with the reader, his attempt to make life art lies beyond the last page of the novel.

When Agathon dies, Peeker accepts his role as successor and brings the tale to a close. Peeker, Gardner suggests, has benefited greatly from Agathon's narrative techniques, and when he relates the story of Agathon's final days to Tuka and her children, he boasts, "The story took a long time to tell. I told it like a poet" (240). Yet having read Agathon's "prison scrolls," Tuka surprises Peeker when she asks if he has any idea " 'how much [of Agathon's tale] is pure fiction.' " In a sense, Agathon may be said to be writing a work similar to *The Sunlight Dialogues*, with himself in the role of the doomed Taggert Hodge, a mad visionary who creates illusions to teach the literal-minded Fred Clumly about alternative ways of seeing the world. Whether the tale Agathon tells is true or not does not matter, for its effect on Peeker and on us is the same. Agathon may fail as a moral artist, but like Grendel and Hodge, his sacrifice leaves Peeker and us with an example of the kind of life we would not wish to emulate and with a desire to apply what we have learned to making our own lives more complete.

Unlike the pathetic Iona, whose single obsession wastes her mind and body (Gardner's reminder that our physical and spiritual selves are not separate), Tuka retains her power and beauty, and judging from Peeker's response to her, we can only conclude that much of what Agathon has related about her is true. Her final words to Peeker and nearly the last words of the novel — " 'Ah, Demodokos, Demodokos! You do me good!' " (243) — bring with them a catharsis similar to the one evoked by the words of James Page's dead wife at the end of *October Light*. Not only does Peeker tremble at what "went through me," but we feel a connectedness too. Agathon's life has mattered not only because of the knowledge he has left behind but also — and perhaps more importantly — because of the people he has "created" for us to know. The same may be said of any artist who celebrates life. The sadness is that Agathon himself never seems to understand the true power he possesses.

The Sunlight Dialogues

In *The Sunlight Dialogues*, the shadowy, ominous stranger who appears in all of Gardner's novels is fully drawn in the character of Taggert Hodge, the Sunlight Man, and with the aid of the Sunlight Man's "different" way of looking at life, Fred Clumly, Gardner's artist/protagonist, moves toward the broader vision he so desperately needs. *The Sunlight Dialogues* is the first of Gardner's lengthy novels and, as other critics have noted, is probably his major work. Gardner's fondness for the novel as a "loose baggy monster" and his admiration for the lengthy works of Faulkner, Melville, and Tolstoy are directly and indirectly noted in *The Sunlight Dialogues*. Unlike *October Light* and *Freddy's Book*, *The Sunlight Dialogues* is truly architectonic in structure, and never is Gardner's use of doubling more apparent than in the saga of Fred Clumly, the Hodge family, and the Sunlight Man who brings them, and the two story lines, together.[6]

Fred Clumly, the aging Batavia police chief, is a familiar figure to Gardner's readers. As with most of Gardner's older protagonists, Clumly despairs over the condition of his life. He is, as his vigils at funerals and his compassion for the Sunlight Man later reveal, a man of feeling. Like James Chandler and Henry Soames, he has a physical flaw, a skin disease, which when combined with his age and obesity render him at first glance a cartoon figure playing at being police chief: "The whiteness, the hairlessness, the oversized nose all gave him

---

6. Gardner, *The Art of Fiction*, 191.

the look of . . . a grublike monster . . . or a man who has slept three nights in the belly of a whale."[7]

Clumly's life, we soon discover, is typical of a career policeman: " 'My job is Law and Order. That's my first job, and if I can't get that one done, the rest will just have to wait. . . . If there's a law on the books, it's my job to see it's enforced' " (23). Clumly thinks of himself, an early chapter title reveals, as the "watchdog of society," yet he is afraid of what is taking place in Batavia and in the world at large. As we might expect of the companion novel to *The Wreckage of Agathon, The Sunlight Dialogues* is permeated with an atmosphere of the sixties, during which Gardner wrote both novels; the Vietnam War, hippies, the sexual revolution, and the civil rights movement make their influences felt even in hamlets like Batavia, New York. Yet the residents of Batavia seem not so much aware of external forces of change as of an internal pressure perhaps arising out of the natural world itself. A random (r)evolutionary stirring of the orderly pastoral Eden is felt as "secret powers at work in the ancient plaster walls, devouring and building, and forces growing and restive in the trees, the very earth itself succinct with spirit" (58). Anxious and disappointed, Clumly is haunted more specifically by the presence of an "ominous stranger," an "intruder": "He heard it distinctly, or felt it through the walls and beams of the house and the dark packed earth below the grass" (17).

As police chief, Clumly knows the threats of change as more than suspicions, intuitions, or feelings. Petty crime is on the rise in Batavia, and when a scarred stranger is arrested for painting *love* on the highway, Clumly's fears and doubts about his life focus on the presence of this bearded prisoner: "Every nerve in his body was jangling because of that prisoner. Or partly that. He'd been nervous for months, to tell the truth; the prisoner was the final straw" (17). The "bearded, disfigured magician," the Sunlight Man, as he is called, turns out to be the stimulus that Clumly needs to rouse himself from the shroud of despair in which he is buried.

The source of Clumly's despair is not only the unsettling demise of Batavia but also a kind of "midlife crisis." At the beginning of the novel, he believes he was trapped by youthful romanticism into marriage with a blind woman: "He'd made a mistake in marrying her, one he might never have made if he'd been a few years older when they met,

7. John Gardner, *The Sunlight Dialogues* (New York, 1972), 6. Further references to this edition will be made in the text.

but his mistake, nevertheless. A mistake he was stuck with" (11). Esther Clumly is, in fact, as ugly as Clumly himself. Drawn and pinched by age, she looks to Clumly like a "dead chicken" in bed, and he has learned to suppress his feelings of disgust if there "were hairs in the food," or "if her slip showed or she smelled of wine" (13). Clumly's vision of his life is a severely limited one: "the years stretched out before him like a cheap hall rug in a strange and unfriendly hotel," and we are told that, like Henry Soames and Peter Mickelsson, "Chief of Police Fred Clumly [has] renounced the world" (13).

Yet Clumly also reflects on a time when his life was not defined by responsibilities to his job and his wife. At odd moments, when the pressures of the present are too much, Clumly escapes into his past, recalling the freedom of his youth aboard a Navy ship: "It was the sea that did it, old and bottomless with mystery, as people say, capable at times of unbelievable rage, and capable, too, of a peace that baffled you. As he'd tried to explain to Mayor Mullen once, to a man locked up in a steel ship, the sea was, well, really something. It *changed* you" (12). The sea is Clumly's personal symbol of innocence and freedom, and memories of his youth only strengthen the feeling that he is now locked into his job, his marriage, and his deteriorating mental and physical condition.

In contrast to Clumly's memories of innocence and freedom on the sea, the central recurring images of the natural world in Clumly's present life are Stony Hill—the Hodge family's former estate—and the Batavia cemetery. It is no accident that the decaying and overgrown Stony Hill, now leased to "Negro tenants," and the resting place for Batavia's dead are so closely intertwined. The sad decline of the Hodges has been likened to the fall of Adam and Eve, with Stony Hill as a once-abundant Eden created by and for Congressman Arthur Hodge, Sr. With the death of the godlike congressman, the remaining members of the clan exist in a kind of purgatory, awaiting either salvation or final condemnation.[8] The eventual suicide of Luke Hodge and the accidental murder of his Uncle Taggert, the Sunlight Man, confirm this fall from grace. By the time Luke's and Hodge's lives end in the final actions of the novel, however, their deaths are meant to be seen not as needless or futile but as sacrificial. In Gardner's carefully woven tapestry of the Hodge family, nearly all members come to terms with themselves. They may not be as aware as Fred Clumly is of

8. Cowart, *Arches and Light*, 69–75.

the resurrection that the Sunlight Man has provided, but they certainly have been brought closer together than they have been since that Edenic time when the congressman held the community in an orderly and respectable union.

The fall of the Hodges coincides with the dissolution of the community, as various factions compete for attention and political favors and create a new morality, so to speak, of which Fred Clumly will have no part. With the once-Edenic little town in chaos, Clumly's only retreat, his pastoral haven, seems to be the cemetery where he is witness to no less than four funerals in the course of the novel. On his first visit, for the funeral of nurseryman Albert Hubbard, Clumly sees the burial ritual as a reward for an orderly life. Such a ritual is most reassuring for Clumly because the underpinnings of his own life, "law and order," seem about to collapse:

> Fred Clumly enjoyed funerals. It was a sad thing to see all one's old friends and relatives slipping away, one after the other, leaving their grown sons and daughters weeping, soberly dabbing at their eyes with their neat white hankies, the grandchildren sitting on the gravestones or standing unwillingly solemn at the side of the grave while they lowered the coffin. But it was pleasant, too, in a mysterious way he couldn't and didn't really want to find words for. There stood the whole family — three, four generations — the living testimonial to the man's having been; all dressed in their finest and at peace with one another; and there stood his business acquaintances and his friends from the church, the school-board he'd once been a member of, all quarrels forgotten; and there stood his friends from the Dairyman's League or Kiwanis or the Owls or the Masons. The coffin rolled silently out of the hearse, and his friends, brothers, sons took the glittering handles and lowered him slowly onto the beams across the hole and then stood back, red-faced from their life's work as truckers or farmers, or sallow-faced from the bank or grocery store or laundry. And there it was, a man's whole life drawn together at last, stilled to a charm, honored and respected, and the minister took off his black hat and prayed, and Clumly prayed, with tears in his eyes and his police cap over his fallen chest, and so, with dignity, the man's life closed, like the book in the minister's hands. (19)

Although Clumly senses the importance of the continuity of life in its steady movement toward death, he has little conviction that his own life has been worthwhile and wonders if death is perhaps the only moment of order left in the modern age. Clumly is also unable to deal with the mutability inherent in the scene at the cemetery. As is usually the case, Gardner's natural world contains the flux of life, positive and negative, chaotic and orderly. Under increasing pressure brought on by the rash of unsolved crimes and by the mayor's insistence on economic efficiency and business acumen in running the police department, Clumly, at this point in the novel, "felt like a man being spied on through a mirror" (34) and is incapable of considering, as James Chandler finally does, that "*order and disorder. These two things are one.*" "A funny business" is all Clumly can think to say at the disintegration of his life and his control over law and order in Batavia.

Despite the comforting sense of closure that Clumly derives from attending funerals, we are not meant to accept his view of death as Gardner's. At the funeral of Clumly's young deputy, Mickey Salvador, who is shot by Nick Slater as Slater and the Sunlight Man escape from the Batavia jail, Clumly finds the same calm and order as at the gravesite of someone like Hubbard, who has died of natural causes: "An untimely end, but the funeral was fitting, and all the dignity of Mickey Salvador's life was there—his mother, weeping, the younger children, the relatives heavy of body and heart, the school friends. *We all go sometime*, Clumly thought. At last, whatever tensions, uncertainties, joys and sorrows warred in the heart, law and order were restored, and there was peace" (380). Clumly's inability to feel sorrow or grief at a life needlessly wasted, however, reveals his pathological view of death. The cruel reality of the young man's murder must be forced upon Clumly and the "fitting order" of the funeral broken when an old, blind Italian woman, Salvador's grandmother, collapses at the gravesite:

> There was an old Italian woman sitting on the ground, her legs splayed out, skirt hiked up to reveal the terrible gray of her thighs above the rolled stocking-tops. . . . She was blind and seemed dazed. When Clumly bent over her she drew back as if alarmed, saying something in Italian—"*uno stormo d'uccelli.*"
> "What?" Clumly said. He glanced at the boy for help.
> "Storm of birds," the boy said. . . .
> "Voli di colombi," she said.
> "Flights of pigeons," the boy said dully, looking down.
> "What's this mean?" Clumly said, but no one answered. The crowd grew nearer to listen.
> "La morte," she said.
> "Death," said the boy.
> She was speaking directly—unmistakably—to Clumly. She began to whisper, and the boy went on translating, quick, toneless, indifferent. "Some will die for uncontrol and animalness and for cruel mastering. Some for violent kindness." She touched Clumly's face—her hands ice-cold—and said a word which the boy did not translate. She repeated it. "*Disanimata.*"
> "What does it mean?" Clumly said.
> The boy looked blank and sullen.
> The others would not say either. (380-81)

The old woman's words give warning to Clumly. By the end of the novel, he has discovered, through the aid of the Sunlight Man and his own wife Esther, the meaning behind this mysterious event. As Gardner has said,

> the real oracle in *The Sunlight Dialogues* is not the Sunlight Man. He's crazy; he's not an oracle at all. But there is an oracle; there's a real ancient sibyl in that novel. When Clumly is at a funeral one day (as usual, he's always going to funerals), an old Italian woman falls down and starts speaking Italian. She gives him oracular statements about the meaning of life and death. Clumly doesn't understand Italian, and the little boy refuses to translate the final oracular statement, which has to do with *disanimata*—"disanimated." But Clumly comes to understand it at the end. He uses it in his mind during the last speech.

Gardner goes on to say that the oracle is a metaphor for "one who sees the totality, the connectedness, and is able to communicate it to other people, to make people see relationships."[9] Just as Stony Hill and the Batavia cemetery contain elements of order and chaos, life and death, death and resurrection, so does each and every human being. Clumly's misreadings of the signs of nature and of the funeral ritual only contribute to his limited vision. As Gardner suggests, and as Clumly eventually learns, a more expansive and accurate vision can be developed, but only through considerable effort and inner conflict, and like great art, it cannot be faked.

Clumly's narrow-mindedness, and in particular his obsession with law and order, poses a challenge to Taggert Hodge. Although the Sunlight Man has returned to Batavia to seek revenge on his father-in-law Clive Paxton, he becomes curiously drawn to Clumly, in much the same way that Clumly is drawn to him. He remembers Clumly as "an officious, sharp-eyed, sharp-witted little man . . . steaming with dangerous conviction. . . . 'A man of principle,' people said, which was to say as inflexible as a chunk of steel, with a heart so cold that if you touched it you'd stick as your fingers stick to iron at twenty below zero" (248–49). But the Sunlight Man sees that Clumly has changed over the years: "He was a puzzle now. . . . It was not that he had mellowed: there was not a hint of that in him. . . . He was, like all his kind, an iron fence; but the fence was not square and neat, it was a labyrinth; and Hodge, in Clumly's presence, felt a mysterious temptation to try his luck in its wanderings" (250).

9. Bellamy, *The New Fiction*, 175–76.

Unlike Clumly, who possesses the benign lunacy of Gardner's true artists, the Sunlight Man is psychotic, driven to violent madness by the patriarchal tyranny of his father and his father-in-law. Reminiscent of the Faulknerian juxtaposition of traditional, aristocratic rule and modern cutthroat capitalism, the power struggle between the Hodges and Clive Paxton, especially after the death of the congressman, apparently divides the town into opposing camps. Paxton, who represents the modern age, is assured of winning control of Batavia, just as Flem Snopes rather easily rises to power in Yoknapatawpha County. Paxton is unwittingly aided in his battle to overthrow the Hodge dynasty by Millie Jewel, whose desire for social position leads her to marry Taggert's brother Will. Her craving for power and her amoral nature destroy the Hodge family's illusions of respectability and order from within.

The psychodrama continues as the brilliant but high-strung Taggert Hodge and Kathleen Paxton fall in love and marry against the wishes of Clive Paxton. The strain is too much for Kathleen, and Hodge soon must give up his law practice in Batavia to follow his mentally ill wife from one psychiatric center to another. Unable to pay the expenses for such treatment and faced with his rich father-in-law's refusal to pay unless the marriage is annulled, Hodge undertakes certain illegal practices to help finance his wife's care.

In contrast to Clumly, who places so much faith in social convention and order, Hodge begins to understand that the law on which he has been nurtured and which he has been practicing is an inflexible system of order and under certain circumstances must be broken. At this point, his quest for freedom begins. Hodge's rage at the artificial values imposed on his life by the past is not fully awakened, however, until Kathleen escapes from an institution, returns to Batavia, and burns down Hodge's house, killing their two sons. Hodge himself is saved only by being blown out of the inferno. He receives "the mark of Cain" from this "baptism by fire" and begins to formulate an elaborate plan of revenge on the Hodges and the Paxtons: "It was not impossible that he was mad. He had earned it, if he was. It felt like the rage of a madman, at times" (246). Eventually—and we are given all of this information through Gardner's beautiful manipulation of plot—we discover that Hodge has killed Clive Paxton and soon becomes indirectly responsible for the deaths of several innocent persons, among them Mickey Salvador.

Like Melville's Ahab, whom Gardner no doubt had in mind as he created the scarred, Satanic hero of *The Sunlight Dialogues*, the Sunlight Man exists outside the laws of civilization: "He'd never been in jail before, he said, and he apparently believed himself set apart by nature from the others—as if by that perhaps unjust and unwarranted, meaningless brand, like the mark of Cain—so that his punishment was more cruel than [the other prisoners'], downright absurd, in fact" (61). And like Ahab, the Sunlight Man is doomed from the start but not eliminated until he provides a valuable lesson for humanity.

As in all of Gardner's novels, the ominous stranger is threatening because he delivers mind- and life-altering information. The possibility of freedom offered by the Sunlight Man tempts Clumly, for despite his resignation to the mechanical winding down of his life, Clumly is nagged by the feeling that there must be more to existence. Clumly's "secret" meetings with the Sunlight Man, a series of four dialogues, are battles of will in which each tries desperately to see the world from inside the other's head.[10] As Clumly struggles to understand how a person could believe "in nothing," the Sunlight Man attempts to demonstrate how Clumly's system of law and order cannot make allowances for the total range of human emotions and conditions. Through their concern and curiosity for one another, they become united in mutual respect by the end of the novel. After the "Dialogue of the Towers," when Clumly finally realizes that abstractions of law must sometimes give way to human conscience, he no longer tries to capture the Sunlight Man. As he lets Hodge drive away in a police cruiser, Clumly asks his deputy Kozlowski, who has been hiding nearby, why he did not interfere. With his reply, Kozlowski recognizes the bond of human compassion and understanding between Clumly and the Sunlight Man that the whole community will soon see: " 'Interfere with which of you?' he said" (634).

It is this striving of the human imagination to create a state of connectedness between people that Gardner establishes as the primary tool for gaining knowledge in *The Sunlight Dialogues*. The Sunlight Man uses the ancient past to reveal to Clumly that any attempt to impose a single absolute order—a single absolute vision—on the world is absurd. "The Sunlight Man," Gardner has said, "can see into all sorts of crazy alternatives, but he finds no order, no coherence in it. He's a

---

10. Morris, *A World of Order and Light*, 71–96. Morris is particularly adept at summarizing the important points of each of the four dialogues.

wild, romantic poet with no hope of God."[11] In the Darwinian terms that Gardner often uses, Hodge possesses the random, chaotic power of artistic imagination but lacks a method for "intense ordering," which true art must have in order to "evolve." Through his magic tricks and philosophical lectures, the Sunlight Man at best only jogs Clumly from his complacent acceptance of law and order and from the belief that his life is a failure. Try as he may, the Sunlight Man has neither the time nor the patience to shake Clumly's firm intuition that " 'higher authorities' " will bring final justice, and he settles on a compromise, accepting Clumly's need for some kind of order in the universe, even though he cannot fathom it himself. " 'I feel friendly toward you, Fred' " (634) are his final words of understanding, ironically echoing Clumly's earliest attempt to coerce him into a confession.

Clumly does not fully comprehend the weight of what he has learned until the Sunlight Man is killed. Gardner elaborates: "Just before his last speech, Clumly looks through a door and sees it's burning inside: he's gotten inside the Sunlight Man's emotions. He fully understands even though he can't make sense of it. At least he has compassion, which is a kind of imagination."[12] And the catalyst for Clumly's expression of this compassion in his speech at the end of the novel is not the dead Taggert Hodge but the living symbol of love, his wife Esther. Like Gardner's other intercessors, Esther draws Clumly back into the world.

Clumly, as Gardner's moral artist, is lost at the beginning of the novel. A realist, he only mirrors the world's state of confusion, and he longs for the past when each man was able to establish a type of absolute order in his own life. The Sunlight Man, an artistic failure, imagines all sorts of fascinating and elaborate plots, but he is not able to affirm any one of them as basically moral. As Gardner has said, "the ability to make up grand images and to thrill the reader is a nice talent, but if it doesn't include love, it's nothing—mere sound brass." If imagination is the key to understanding and accepting oneself and others—to achieving wholeness—then "the two characters who have the most imagination in the novel are Clumly and Mrs. Clumly, because they can see into other people's minds. With his little mole's intelligence, Clumly stares at the Sunlight Man and tries to understand

---

11. Quoted in Bellamy, *The New Fiction*, 188.
12. Quoted in *ibid.*, 188.

him. He really tries to understand the principle of evil by empathizing with it."[13]

Gardner may somewhat overstate his case, but when Clumly does come to this understanding of the evil that exists in all of us, he is able to forgive not only himself but also the Sunlight Man and all of the people of Batavia. In the midst of this revelation, as he gives his final speech before the Dairyman's League, he realizes that his long-suffering wife Esther is the real basis of his salvation, for Esther affirms the importance of love. Just as the Sunlight Man becomes a sacrificial figure for the community, so Esther sacrifices her life for Clumly.

Esther Clumly's world, like her husband's, is quite limited. Deprived of eyesight, she lives in her imagination. For her, Fred Clumly is a saint because when she was young he loved her and stayed with her even after an operation on her eyes left her completely blind. When she discovered that the operation was a failure, she thought of committing suicide, "for in her mind at least there was dignity yet, and romance and poetry and revenge" (276). She could have preserved her dignity, and Fred's, she believes, if she had ended her life those long years ago: "She wanted to sacrifice, be crucified for him, for in a part of her heart she was innocent and childlike and pure as beryl, but the other part of her laughed at that and said *Esther, you stick with me and we'll make us a life.* Well, what could she do? She had given in" (277).

Each day Esther goes over and over her life, trying to convince herself that she is selfish for thinking about lost opportunities: "Surely no one in the world has ever been more sick with self-pity" (295). Blindness, she believes, destroyed the "artistic" life that had been somehow promised her: "I was a person of talent, Esther Clumly was saying to herself. I could carry a tune . . . and I was a quick learner. I could have written poetry" (294). But worst of all, Esther feels, blindness has robbed her of the ability to love and be loved: "Eyes are the windows of the soul; something like that. . . . Then a woman without eyes cannot be loved. Her soul is sealed up like a vicious dog chained in a cellar, and little by little it goes mad, or loses spirit and eventually dies, and lucky to escape, at that. My only hope must be giving my love to others, and I've failed" (295). Esther's guilt arises from the sole responsibility she takes for the boredom of her present life with Clumly. She excuses her husband for his lack of affection because she expects

13. Quoted in *ibid.*, 188.

nothing from him. The extent of her sacrifice, her love for him, is revealed when she attributes all of Clumly's strange behavior and actions—his "madness"—to a plot against him by the mayor and other city officials. In the chapter "Love and Duty," Esther, in an act of great courage, reports her fears to Officer Miller at the police station and presents him with the tapes of Clumly's dialogues with the Sunlight Man. When Miller, out of loyalty, refuses to listen to the tapes without Clumly's knowledge, Esther sees her act of love as merely another failure and betrayal: "When [Miller] spoke his voice was too even, and she knew that, whatever it was she'd done, she had ruined her husband and had made it impossible for even Miller to help him now" (542). What Esther does not realize is the enormity of her own compassion and her ability to absorb all of the pain and problems of her life and of Clumly's as well. As Gardner has acknowledged, Esther Clumly is "the Beatrice of *The Sunlight Dialogues*. She guides everybody because she loves. This is the kind of imagination which holds the world together. The ability to be patient, to be tolerant, to try to understand and empathize, is the highest kind of imagination."[14] Esther helps her husband move toward the kind of all-embracing vision that an artist uses to strive for aesthetic wholeness.

As he begins his speech at the end of the novel, Clumly is informed of the death of the Sunlight Man. In his agony—for he has "seen" the fire in the Sunlight Man's mind—Clumly conjures up a vision of Esther and realizes that he must, as best he can, tell the truth about himself, tell all he has learned. His speech to the Dairy League meeting, which most of the prominent townspeople regularly attend, sets up the epiphanic gathering that occurs in all of Gardner's novels. At the gathering, Clumly tries for the first time to put into words what he has learned.[15] Clumly literally "speaks his mind." Gardner's rendering of the speech is perfect, for it summarizes the spontaneous, sometimes vague, yet often insightful nature of Clumly's, and our own, movement toward understanding in the novel:

14. Quoted in *ibid.*, 188–89.
15. *Encyclopedia of Philosophy*, I, 31. Croce argues, and Collingwood appears to agree, that when we clarify "impressions" taken from the raw sensory data of the world, they are "expressed" as what we call "intuitions." To "express," in this subjective sense, apart from any external physical activity, is to create art. For Croce and Collingwood, art is feeling translated into language. Clumly's expression of what he has discovered suggests that he is an artist of sorts.

"We see people that are lucky and that live their whole lives in the shelter of Law and Order . . . and one of these days they die and we go to their funeral. . . . All the man's family there, standing around the grave, and his grandchildren standing there all dressed up, and his friends standing around crying and wringing their hankies and remembering all he ever said to them or did for them. That's order. That's right to the heart of what Order is. Because all his life he obeyed the law. And now all the people that ever knew him come together and give him the dignity of that last final order." (669)

This "coming together" of one person with the community of friends and neighbors, Clumly implies, should be the force that holds life together.

Clumly goes on to reiterate his theory about death as an absolute: " 'It's a beautiful thing, the order in a man's life, and sometimes you wonder if that's not the only time it's visible, after he's dead and it's there beside his grave' " (669). Certainly this is the kind of order with which his audience is most familiar, for most of them have observed the funerals of fellow townspeople with Clumly. But when Clumly thinks of the death of the Sunlight Man—a man outside the established order of things—he begins to feel a kind of "connectedness" that transcends the dictates of society, and for the first time he sees death for what it is—a horrible abyss toward which we are all moving. Clumly slowly realizes that only love and compassion, the true sources of community strength, can hold off for a while the end of all things.

In speaking about the death of the Sunlight Man, shot by Clumly's deputy as he tried to give himself up, Clumly bravely attempts to put this new awareness into words: " 'Sometimes it seems as if there *is* no justice. A man dies—shot through the heart . . . a man dies and you think, *Lord, Lord, where is your justice*? Was that what he was born for?' " (668). In summarizing the character and brilliance of the Sunlight Man, Clumly makes his audience, not yet aware that Taggert Hodge is the Sunlight Man, come to see that they must accept some of the blame for the accidental death and for all injustice caused by inflexible and arbitrary law and order. Their reaction, however, is understandable: "They sat motionless as rocks and stumps, as if they . . . were aware that the angel was there, or the angel's hand, outrageously condemning them for doing nothing wrong" (669). Clumly, of course, is also speaking about the sympathetic relationship that should exist between all human beings and about the Sunlight Man as a member of the human community. He admits for the first time that " 'we may be wrong about the whole thing' " (672), and by suggesting that one person's or one community's idea of law and order and justice may not be applicable to all people, Clumly reveals his intuitive understanding of the changing nature of a world in which all rational systems of order eventually disintegrate.

Nevertheless, Clumly goes on to say, the Sunlight Man lived outside of their mutually agreed-upon law and order, which does sustain them momentarily, and because he chose or was forced to set himself apart, "we can't honor him with the kind of order we give to those others" who do live within the bounds of acceptable social behavior. Clumly understands and sympathizes with the Sunlight Man's alternate vision, but he cannot dismiss entirely the values on which he has based his own life. Clumly realizes, even before the Sunlight Man does, that "absolute freedom" does not and cannot exist any more than absolute order can. As Gardner's moral artist, Clumly, in the course of events in the novel, tests each traditional community-held value and finds some of them lacking. Through the process of testing these values, under all sorts of pressures, Clumly discovers that one must have faith not in abstractions — "the law" — but in the people who make the laws — the community itself.

Clumly concludes his rather disjointed speech by stating that the best a human being can do is keep an open mind and be ready to act according to the laws " 'as best we're able to see them.' " The intensity of his feeling for his fellow human beings at this moment is so great that it brings to mind the image of the only person he knows who epitomizes the potential understanding and love within the human heart — his wife Esther: "His face strained, struggling to get it all clearer, if only to himself. He thought of Esther. 'Now there's a fine model for us all,' he said emphatically, pointing at the ceiling. . . . 'Blessed are the meek, by which I mean all of us, including the Sunlight Man,' he said. 'God be kind to all Good Samaritans and also bad ones. For of such is the Kingdom of Heaven' " (672). On the applause that follows, Gardner has Clumly borne up "to where the light was brighter than sun-filled clouds, disanimated and holy" (673). The old Italian woman's words are realized. For Gardner, the true artist's duty is to use his imagination to expose and authenticate the necessity for love and its corollaries compassion and forgiveness, the only means of achieving aesthetic wholeness. Like Henry Soames, Fred Clumly, with the sacrifice of the Sunlight Man and the inspiration provided by his wife Esther, comes to embrace the "holiness of all things."

4

The Monster as Artist
Grendel
and *Freddy's Book*

I'm talking mainly—though not exclusively—
about works of fiction that are moral in their
process. . . . Good works of fiction study values
by testing them in imagined/real situations,
testing them hard, being absolutely fair to both
sides.—JOHN GARDNER

Grendel

So much has been written about *Grendel* that dealing with Gardner's
slim retelling of the Old English epic *Beowulf* from the monster's
point of view seems a little repetitious. The careful structuring of the
novel, based on the twelve signs of the zodiac and the twelve Aristote-
lian virtues, has been thoroughly explicated. In fact, there has been an
overemphasis on Gardner's structural devices and metafictional techniques, the sheer cleverness of which accounts for much of the novel's
popularity among critics, reviewers, and general readers. More recent
studies have begun to focus on character and ideas in the novel. The
most interesting reading of *Grendel*, for my purposes, is David Cowart's argument that Grendel is an artist, relating his own story in a series of flashbacks after he has learned his narrative art from encounters with the Shaper. Grendel's storytelling powers increase, Cowart
suggests, as the novel progresses, so that we see more sophisticated fictional, poetic, and dramatic techniques displayed as the novel reaches
its climax.[1]

1. Strehle, "John Gardner's Novels: Affirmation and the Alien," 86–96; Craig J.
Stromme, "The Twelve Chapters of *Grendel*," *Critique*, XX (1978), 83–92; David
Minugh, "John Gardner Constructs *Grendel*'s Universe," *Studies in English Philology, Linguistics, and Literature: Presented to Alarik Rynell (March 7, 1978)*, in Mats
Ryden and Lennart A. Bjork (eds.), *Stockholm Studies in English*, XLVI (Stockholm, 1978), 125–41; Elizabeth Larson, "The Creative Act: An Analysis of Systems
in *Grendel*," in Mendez-Egle (ed.), *John Gardner: True Art, Moral Art*, 36–51; Morris, *A World of Order and Light*, 51–70; Cowart, *Arches and Light*, 38–56.

If Cowart is correct about Grendel's narrative powers—and my entire approach to Gardner's novels suggests that he is—we should also note Gardner's unusual use of the first-person point of view. In nearly all of his novels, Gardner refuses to limit his narrative and insists on exploring all of his major characters' thoughts and beliefs, with the understanding that no one character is all good or all bad. Why then does he choose for *Grendel* a point of view that he has said presents "portraits or comic cartoons of the artist" and little more? An argument could be made that because Gardner is dealing with a tale as familiar as *Beowulf*, which has already been narrated from a human point of view, he feels no need to cover the same territory again and prefers instead Grendel's alternate perspective of these events. Gardner has said "Grendel is a monster, and living in the first person because we're all in some sense monsters, trapped in our own language and habits of emotion." But Gardner's use of the first person is more than just an interesting technique. Grendel's relation of his encounters with human beings is similar to Jack Winesap's "unfinished" first-person narrative of his encounter with a monster, a "potential Grendel," in *Freddy's Book*. Grendel, like Winesap, is a failed artist, and like another of Gardner's failed artists, Agathon, he dominates the novel in which he appears. Even if we had no other evidence, the use of the first-person point of view in the tales of Grendel, Agathon, Winesap, and Peeker reveals their weaknesses and limitations as moral artists.[2]

Gardner's use of the first person for Grendel's narrative increases our sense of the monster's isolation. Unlike his mother, who is truly bestial but not without some inherent virtue, Grendel has "evolved" a human intellect. He thinks and speaks a kind of human language, and is moved by the power of the Shaper's poetry. He no longer fits into the underground world of the "mere" yet cannot ever gain entry into the world of men and women. Unlike Gardner's other "monster," Freddy Agaard, who chooses isolation to avoid the cruelty and callousness of "normal" people, Grendel is forced into isolation by his bestial appearance and limited imagination. Whereas Freddy discovers that art is the best means of dealing with his giantism—he uses both intellect and feeling to develop a piece of "moral fiction"—Grendel is not able to move beyond his fascination with language itself.

2. John Gardner, *On Becoming A Novelist* (New York, 1983), 29; Ferguson, *et al.*, "John Gardner: The Art of Fiction LXXIII," 44.

Very early in his narrative, he admits his entrapment: "Talking, talking, spinning a spell, pale skin of words that closes me in like a
coffin."[3] As Gregory Morris has suggested, Grendel never reckons with
the power of the imagination that moves human beings beyond the
"web" of language and the static nature of facts. Freddy's use of the
third-person point of view for "King Gustav and the Devil" suggests the
possibility of "resurrection," but Grendel's reliance on the first person
can only mean doom. We identify with Grendel because of this intimate
point of view, but also because we already know the outcome of *Beowulf*. With Gardner's careful manipulation, the pull of the first-person
narrative working on us and the pull of entropy that Grendel feels become one, moving inexorably toward Grendel's death.

As the protagonist of the novel, Grendel possesses several characteristics of Gardner's moral artists: like Henry Soames and James
Page, he is filled with a desperate and seething rage; like James
Chandler and Peter Mickelsson, he comes to rely too heavily upon
reason to make sense of the world; and like Gerald Craine in the incomplete *Shadows*, he embraces a "system" by which to live. Yet these
characteristics hinder any chance for redemption or reintegration.[4]
Obviously, Grendel is the "monster" in each of us, but for Gardner the
darker side of human nature is not only a bestial, raging id but also a
limited intellectual and imaginative vision. With an early awareness
that entropy rules the universe and bored with "the terrible sameness"
of things, Grendel, with such a limited vision, misreads the world and
is responsible for his own movement toward chaos and violent death.
Because of his physical and mental isolation, Grendel, unlike most of
Gardner's protagonists, never emerges from the Dantean darkness.
The Shaper and Queen Wealtheow bring Grendel to an awareness of
his terrible situation, but he is never able to act on their examples.

Grendel is interesting to my study because we are allowed to see him
develop the philosophical and artistic vision that is so wrongheaded.
He was not always, he tells us, a threatening monster, "world rim-
walker," "Wrecker of Kings." Early in his life, like most of us, he was
unsure about what the world held for him and wondered at his own
existence: "I lived those years, as do all young things, in a spell. Like a
puppy nipping, playfully growling preparing for battle with wolves"
(16). Gradually he became aware of himself as an entity separate from

3. John Gardner, *Grendel* (New York, 1971), 15. Further references to this edition will
be made in the text.
4. Harvey, "Where Philosophy and Fiction Meet," 75.

his mother, and this self-consciousness also contained the knowledge of death. Although he retreats to his mother's arms in fear, eventually he comes to understand that he must deal with a "world . . . suddenly transformed, fixed like a rose with a nail through it, space hurtling coldly out from me in all directions" (17–18). Nevertheless, he feels as though he has been born to some special destiny he cannot as yet comprehend. His new awareness culminates in a first brush with death. One leg accidentally trapped in a crotch between two old tree trunks, he is attacked first by a bull and then by men. Like many artists, Grendel at an early age is forced to deal with a brutal and meaningless reality: "I seemed to see the whole universe, even the sun and sky, leaping forward, then sinking away again, decomposing. Everything was wreckage, putrefaction" (19). Although this time he is saved from death by his mother, Grendel becomes like the artist who stares into the abyss and denies forever after that there is anything more to living. Grendel's problem, and his choice, like that of Gardner's other artist/ protagonists, becomes how best to deal with such a world.

Most of Gardner's protagonists retreat into nature to try and recover some semblance of the order they knew as children growing up on their fathers' farms or in small towns, but Grendel never emerges from the natural world of his origin. In addition, this environment is far removed from the pastoral havens of Gardner's other protagonists. The darker side of nature—its brutality, mystery, and instinctual urgings—is never more fully realized than in *Grendel*. Outside the walls of Hrothgar's meadhall, the dense primeval forests hide wolves, snakes, and even human predators, not to mention the dragon and Grendel himself. To survive in such a world, human beings develop various systems and rituals, but, as Gardner is fond of pointing out, all systems and rituals are subject to change. Certain values arising from human interaction, however, appear to be, if not absolute, at least enduring. Love, compassion, and a sense of community, all of which require a sympathetic imagination, can, if strengthened by art, insure human survival. The ability to generate such "connectedness" is a power that Grendel is unable to comprehend. Grendel sees only danger in the unpredictable nature of human action motivated sometimes by intellect, sometimes by feeling, and sometimes by both, but Gardner wants us to realize that this very unpredictability allows for the possibility of a more interesting and hopeful existence.

When Grendel first encounters people, he sees them as only fellow-creatures of the bull that nearly kills him and of the animals on which he and his mother prey for food. When he tries to communicate with them, however, he discovers that he is "dealing with no dull mechanical bull but with thinking creatures, pattern makers, the most dangerous things I'd ever met" (27). When Hrothgar and his men assault him with arrows and axes, Grendel's response is understandable—" 'You're all crazy,' I bellowed, 'you're all insane!' " (27). For a moment, Hrothgar and his men become Grendel-like monsters, attacking something they don't understand, and we respond sympathetically to Grendel's cries.

Despite all of the "artistic" skills he develops, Grendel never rises above this initial gut-wrenching cry—" 'You're all crazy' "—and from this feeling he develops his "theory of being": " I understood that the world was nothing: a mechanical chaos of casual, brute enmity on which we stupidly impose our hopes and fears. I understood that, finally and absolutely, I alone exist. All the rest, I saw, is merely what pushes me, or what I push against. . . . I create the whole universe, blink by blink" (21–22). As Gregory Morris has stated, Grendel "is correct in thinking that we 'create the whole universe, blink by blink'; he goes wrong, however, in ignoring the imaginative power of such a thought and act."[5] Grendel never seems to realize that if he does create the universe, he has the power to make choices other than the "monstrous ones" offered by an existential vision. Rather than plunging into the abyss or satisfying his rage by becoming the "Wrecker of Kings," he has the alternative of learning from his observations of the human community and its moral artist, the Shaper. Grendel is genuinely moved by the power of imaginative regeneration arising out of the Shaper's art (and we see the influence in the tale Grendel tells), but he chooses nevertheless to follow the dragon's advice and become the antithesis of the Shaper. In doing so, he creates a world based on a system of thought rather than on the more flexible imaginative vision of the artist, and moves predictably toward his own death. Since we know the outcome of *Beowulf*, our feeling that fate (the plot) has decreed Grendel's death may obscure the fact that he actually has a choice in how to live his life. But, as Gardner has said, even a monster has a chance at redemption, and although Gardner's failed artists—Viola Staley, Agathon, George Loomis, Taggert Hodge, Bishop Brask—cannot save themselves, they at least realize the possibility of an aesthetically whole vision as they sacrifice themselves for the benefit of the moral artists.

5. Morris, *A World of Order and Light*, 57.

Certainly the humans in *Grendel* are not the most admirable of creatures. They reveal their hypocritical natures again and again in political maneuvers and personal confrontations, and further darken Grendel's view of the world. They are often as trapped and manipulated by language as Grendel eventually is himself, and their appetite for killing appalls even the man-eating monster, who admits, "I was sickened, if only at the waste of it" (36). But with the Shaper's arrival at Hrothgar's Hall, human beings for short periods of time seem able to rise above their "monstrous" behavior. The language of the Shaper's poetry and songs manipulates, to be sure, like the language of a politician or of the dragon — all three offer their advice only "for a price" — but what makes the Shaper's language different is that it changes minds for the "good." By "transmuting" the world, the Shaper inspires and encourages people to press on with life, even in the face of chaos and death: "The man had changed the world, had torn up the past by its thick, gnarled roots and had transmitted it, and they, who knew the truth, remembered it his way — and so did I" (43). Even if, as Gardner has said, the Shaper is "a wonderful hack, a noble hack," the evenings spent under his spell at Hrothgar's Hall are the important gatherings of *Grendel* during which impasses are broken, decisions are made, and history is changed.[6] Even Grendel, who attends these meetings by peering through a chink in the wall, emerges charged with new emotion. Only in art, Gardner reveals, does the highest embodiment take place.

After hearing the Shaper's poetry for the first time, Grendel feels a "split" between his unyielding intellect, which tells him the world is a "mechanical chaos," and his raging feelings, which suggest there is more to life than he, as a member of "the terrible race God cursed," can ever enjoy. Grendel fails to understand that all human beings (as well as thinking monsters) belong to the race of Cain, and that human beings share his feelings of isolation, fear, and guilt. In his search for truth, Grendel finds it easier to allow the dragon to reinforce his initial wrongheadedness than to abandon the value system he has already established. Since Grendel lacks imagination, he cannot distinguish between the manipulation of language for good (the Shaper's poetry) and the manipulation of language for evil (the dragon's philosophical argument). He merely senses the power of language itself and embraces it. He finds the dragon's "logic" more convincing only because the

6. Winther, "An Interview with John Gardner," 514.

dragon's physical presence is so overwhelming and because the dragon's "visions" support his own "preconscious" notions of what life is.

The dragon, who claims to see past, present, and future all at once, represents the darkness and confusion Grendel feels throughout his life. Like the philosophers and artists whom Gardner so often condemns, the dragon encourages the despairing Grendel in his narrow-minded deductions about life. Human beings, the dragon says, rely on " 'simple facts in isolation, and facts to connect them. . . . But there are no such facts.' " The role of a strange creature like the Shaper is to provide " 'an illusion of reality' " at times when human beings begin to sense " 'that all they live by is nonsense. . . . That's where the Shaper saves them . . . puts together all their facts with a gluey whine of connectedness' " (64–65). The reality of the situation, the dragon argues, is that Grendel's very bestiality makes him a greater artist than the Shaper. The dragon encourages Grendel to become an artist of darkness, antithesis of the Shaper, because Grendel's bestial nature reminds human beings of their true condition. Through his "destructive art," the dragon argues, Grendel can force order into what would otherwise be a chaotic world: " 'You improve them my boy! Can't you see that yourself? You stimulate them! You make them think and scheme. You drive them to poetry, science, religion, all that makes them what they are for as long as they last. You are, so to speak, the brute existent by which they learn to define themselves. The exile, captivity, death they shrink from — the blunt facts of their mortality, their abandonment — that's what you make them recognize, embrace! You *are* mankind, or man's condition' " (72–73).

After his talk with the dragon, Grendel feels a greater sense of purpose. Like most of Gardner's protagonists, he emerges from his isolation and reenters the community. The irony, of course, is that Grendel's Satanic advisor, unlike Clumly's Sunlight Man or Peeker's Agathon, is not a doomed "teacher" who sacrifices so that the protagonist may gain a higher level of perception and understanding and make a greater art of his life. The dragon sacrifices nothing and sees only what he wants to see. Like the Devil in *Freddy's Book*, the dragon is an aspect of human nature that cannot be ignored but should not be trusted. The dragon, like the Devil, may eventually be slain, but his attitude and way of seeing continue to influence all of us, for all dragons and devils attest to the darker powers of human imagination.

Grendel comes away from his visit to the dragon with a stronger sense of himself: "I had become something, as if born again I had hung between possibilities before, between the old truths I knew and the heart-sucking conjuring tricks of the Shaper; now that was passed: I was Grendel, Ruiner of Meadhalls, Wrecker of Kings" (80). As an artist, Grendel finally discovers his own "style" and "material," but what he makes of his life is a selfish art. He gains great fame among men but little else. As Gardner has said, "Ultimately it comes down to, are you making or are you destroying? If you try very hard to create ways of living, create dreams of what is possible, then you win. If you don't, you may make a fortune in ten years, but you're not going to be read in twenty years, and that's that."[7] Grendel's life as a work of art can only be second-rate.

Once Grendel describes this achievement of his "artistic identity," he shifts from the account of how he became an artist to detailed observations of Hrothgar's people and the effects of his "art" upon them. Grendel's style and technique in storytelling also become more complex at this point in the novel.

Aware of his own invincibility, Grendel soon becomes bored with merely terrorizing the meadhall and resorts to game-playing in order to revel in his domination of Hrothgar's men. Grendel's refusal to kill Unferth, for instance, not only denies him a heroic death but also humiliates him in front of his fellow thanes. In this scene, Gardner presents a contrast of artistic visions. Grendel's art has taken a new direction, and in his treatment of Unferth, he is like the contemporary writer who makes fun of his hero, strips him of all dignity, reduces him to an animal-like state, and then argues that this is the human condition. Even as he faces the death that will not come, however, Unferth counters Grendel's game-playing by arguing that heroism is more than mere poetic language: " 'The hero sees values beyond what's possible. That's the *nature* of a hero. It kills him, of course, ultimately. But it makes the whole struggle of humanity worthwhile' " (89). This is the kind of vision Gardner's moral artist possesses, and the kind of vision Grendel rejects. Just as the moral artist creates on one level to assuage feelings of guilt or fear, Unferth seeks a hero's death because he is literally a Cain-figure, having killed his brother. Grendel's refusal to allow him a redeeming and heroic death only increases Unferth's feelings of guilt and shame, but what Unferth does not understand is that by continuing to live in the shadow of the darker vision repre-

---

7. Ferguson, *et al.*, "John Gardner: The Art of Fiction LXXIII," 70.

sented by Grendel, he becomes more of a hero, for, despite his suffering, Unferth endures.

Only the coming of a queen into Hrothgar's Hall saves Unferth and reduces Grendel's power. In keeping with the medieval (and fairy-tale) nature of Gardner's narrative, Wealtheow is a stereotype of the virtuous princess. Her beauty is such that she "tore [Grendel] apart as once the Shaper's song had done" (100). Her sacrifice in becoming Hrothgar's queen saves her people from slaughter at the hands of Hrothgar's men and unites rival kingdoms. Her presence at Hrothgar's Hall seems to bring internal peace as well, for she reconciles conflicts among the men and releases Unferth, who is "hunched, bitterly smiling . . . ugly as a spider," from his misery: "The queen smiled. Impossibly, like roses blooming in the heart of December, she said, 'That's past.' And it was. The demon was exorcised. I saw his hands unclench, relax" (104). The queen also inspires the Shaper to sing about "things that had never crossed his mind before: comfort, beauty, a wisdom softer, more permanent, than Hrothgar's" (103). Under the "feminizing influence" of Wealtheow, the gatherings in the meadhall become even more significant for Hrothgar and his people, and perhaps for Grendel, too.

Wealtheow's actions remind Grendel of his own mother's "mindless love," and the queen's power is nearly as great as the Shaper's: "In my mind I watched her freckled hand move on the old man's arm as once I'd listened to the sigh of the Shaper's harp" (108). Sadly, her power as an intercessor is not great enough to help Grendel, and his attack on her is an attempt to "expose" her, literally and figuratively (109–110). Grendel's obsession with the physical—with facts, with things as they are—cripples his imagination. By spreading the queen's legs for all the world to see, Grendel thinks he has "revealed" the illusion of her power—she is after all only flesh. He makes the same mistake again when the Shaper dies. Because the poet's songs help establish Grendel's reputation as "Wrecker of Meadhalls," Grendel worries that the old man's death may somehow diminish his legendary reputation. What Grendel never realizes is that the queen and the Shaper are not aberrations of human nature, for we all possess some of the power of the Shaper's imagination and some of the strength of Wealtheow's love. Cultivation of these "virtues" only strengthens the sense of connectedness between us.

As Grendel sinks into torpor, bored with the "terrible sameness" of things (the state of mind in which we find him at the beginning of the novel), he begins to feel as though "something is coming, strange as spring," and confesses, "I am afraid" (126). The ominous stirrings that accompany each new spring eventually are transferred to the arrival of Beowulf: "He had a strange face that, little by little, grew unsettling to me" (154). Gardner adds to the ominousness of Beowulf's presence by never naming him in the novel. Despite his premonition of disaster, Grendel enters willingly into combat with the gigantic stranger, for Grendel, like the Devil in *Freddy's Book*, has concluded that tedium is the worst pain. Grendel has also never moved beyond his initial judgment of human beings, for he tells us that the look in Beowulf's eyes is "insane." Beowulf's insanity, however, is but the moral artist or hero's glimpse of "possibilities." Obviously, Grendel's "vision" is weaker than Beowulf's, and the contest between the two is no contest at all. Unlike Unferth's conscience, Beowulf's "grip" is not hindered by guilt, fear, or shame; it contains a power and a strength as great as the dragon's: "He has wings. Is it possible? And yet it's true: out of his shoulders come terrible fiery wings" (169). Because Grendel "sees" Beowulf as the dragon, some critics have taken this passage as further evidence of the dragon's influence on Grendel's view of life, but I think the lines suggest the "saving grace" of Beowulf's power, the value he brings as an ominous stranger. Angels, too, have wings, and Beowulf's become, for Grendel, "blinding white" as he drives the dying monster from the meadhall. We should also recall that when Grendel first senses Beowulf's coming, he connects it in some way not with the dragon but with children making angel wings in the snow. Beowulf suggests that a "resurrection" will come—"*Time is the mind, the hand that makes (fingers on harpstrings, hero-swords, the acts, the eyes of queens). By that I kill you*" (170)—for his words recall the great artistic powers for unification and healing possessed by the Shaper, the queen, and even himself, the hero.[8]

Grendel, as a failed artist, cannot take part in such a resurrection, and so he moves off to die alone in the dark. Although he denies to the very end that his death is anything more than an accident, his final words—"'Poor Grendel's had an accident. *So may you all*'" (174)—suggest two other, more significant levels of meaning. Grendel's accident is a result of his blindness to the power of saving art. With life draining from him, Grendel cannot think through his experience with Beowulf, but he does, I believe, understand his error on a subcon-

8. *Ibid.*, 44–45.

scious level. We see such an understanding in his vision of Beowulf with wings and in the relief he feels immediately after he flees from the meadhall. *"Is it joy I feel?"* he wonders as other animals gather to watch him die, and into their eyes he projects the "evil, incredibly stupid" joy at destruction he has often felt, the mistaken vision he has possessed. His last wish carries not only a curse but also a revelation that the Shaper, Queen Wealtheow, and Beowulf have given him. Grendel's final words must also echo Gardner's own wish, for certainly he hopes that readers will learn from Grendel's errors and take advantage of the possibilities for resurrection Grendel is offered but cannot accept. "In the end of the novel," Gardner has said, "Grendel is the real poet"; "nothing the Shaper sings is as powerful . . . as the best poetry of Grendel," but only because Grendel's "accident" moves the reader, not Grendel, closer to an aesthetically satisfying vision of life.[9]

Freddy's Book

After the novel-within-a-novel structure of Gardner's *October Light*, the dual novella structure of *Freddy's Book* should not have come as a surprise to reviewers, who were also aided in their assessments by Gardner's *On Moral Fiction*, published two years before *Freddy's Book*. Yet even those who understood the parody of contemporary fiction interspersed among the pages of *October Light*'s main storyline and who were sympathetic with the thrust of *On Moral Fiction* thought *Freddy's Book* a failure because it does not return to the opening tale of Jack Winesap after he (and the reader) has read "King Gustav and the Devil," Freddy Agaard's novella.[10]

Those critics who have taken the time to reflect on *Freddy's Book*, however, have pointed to several ways the two novellas function as a complete novel and as a successful addition to Gardner's canon of moral fiction. Despite its leap from twentieth-century Madison, Wisconsin, to sixteenth-century Sweden, *Freddy's Book* has been read as a gradual progression from reality into fantasy, from confinement into freedom, and from failed historical visions to a successful one. The structure of *Freddy's Book* can also be explained in terms of character development, for the characters within the first novella, "Freddy," have counterparts within the second, "King Gustav and the Devil." The emphasis on character as a unifier is in keeping with Gardner's in-

---

9. Winther, "An Interview with John Gardner," 514.
10. Morace, *John Gardner: An Annotated Secondary Bibliography,* 164–86.

sistence that character should be of prime importance in any work of fiction.[11]

Although Gardner's artist/protagonist appears within each novella and his minor artists abound, the difficulty in distinguishing between them arises from our usual perception of plot in Gardner's novels as a linear vehicle with a definite closure. Because we do not "see" Jack Winesap's, or Sven Agaard's, or Freddy Agaard's reintegration, as we do those of most of Gardner's protagonists and as we do Lars-Goren's, the novella "Freddy" has been called open-ended or unfinished. I would like to argue, however, that "Freddy," like "King Gustav," is complete, and that Gardner, in providing us with one moral artist, Freddy, has no need to develop another in the character of Jack Winesap. Winesap's first-person narration of "Freddy" is clear evidence that Gardner does not intend for us to take the gregarious professor too seriously. Gardner, we should recall, distrusts first-person point of view because it restricts character development, and he uses first person only in those novels — *Grendel* and *The Wreckage of Agathon* — in which the protagonists never achieve reintegration. Winesap's encounter with Freddy and Professor Agaard, although it makes Winesap angry and guilty, does not approach the kind of epiphanic series of experiences that normally lead to a protagonist's attainment of aesthetic wholeness. A careful look at Gardner's pairing and development of characters will make this notion much clearer.

In each of the two novellas, Gardner gives us three main characters (with the exception of the Devil who is, after all, "mere stench and black air") whose relationships with one another move the plot forward. The debate over history between Jack Winesap, psychohistorian, and Professor Sven Agaard, an old-school Scandinavianist, has been seen as the conflict between traditional and contemporary values present in all of Gardner's fiction. Although Gregory Morris has argued that Agaard's view is the "moral" one, I agree with David Cowart that neither Agaard nor Winesap is to be admired for his philosophical or ethical views.[12] If we think of the novel as process, neither extreme view is to be embraced. Only a careful working out of the best of each set of values — which in this case define approaches to writing history — will provide

---

11. Morris, *A World of Order and Light*, 167–83; Robert A. Morace, "*Freddy's Book*, Moral Fiction, and Writing as a Mode of Thought," *Modern Fiction Studies*, XXIX (Summer, 1983), 201–12; Cowart, *Arches and Light*, 148–64; Gardner, *The Art of Fiction*, 6.

12. Morris, *A World of Order and Light*, 170; Cowart, *Arches and Light*, 150.

what is necessary to achieve lasting success. Although we don't see this process in "Freddy," it is apparent from "King Gustav and the Devil" that Freddy Agaard has already entertained and extracted from the writings of his father and Jack Winesap, even before their debate takes place, the tools necessary to create a satisfying work of moral fiction. In the process of writing his book, as Cowart has said, Freddy has discovered that the best historian is the moral artist.

Freddy the "monster" as moral artist is probably Gardner's joke on those who attacked him for insisting on a moral view in an age when absurdity, chaos, and nihilism better define the world. As an "enlarged" caricature of Gardner, Freddy is a man-out-of-time. Just as Gardner's philosophy of fiction writing would have gained him admiration in the nineteenth century, so Freddy's physical size (as it does in the case of his creation, the knight Lars-Goren Bergquist) would have made him a hero in sixteenth-century Sweden. Freddy has been driven to the edge of despair and madness, but he has suffered longer than most of Gardner's protagonists because of his "freakishness" and, we might suspect, because of his father's stubborn attitude. (That Freddy seems to have no mother probably contributes to his isolation, since in Gardner's fiction women are often mediating influences between male protagonists and the world.) Freddy is, in fact, a "potential Grendel," and Jack Winesap sees the physical evidence of Freddy's rage and power in the smashed walls of the servant's room.[13] Freddy isolates himself from the world by "locking it out," but luckily he is able to retreat to his father's library and eventually discovers his own abilities as an artist. He is saved from despair by his work, but as a moral artist he must also emerge from his isolation to make contact with the world again. His father, by inviting Jack Winesap to meet Freddy, and Winesap, by accepting, offer Freddy that opportunity; and Freddy, in letting Winesap read his book "King Gustav and the Devil," takes it.

When Gardner's novel opens, Freddy already knows what Lars-Goren learns—that the only source of good and evil is human nature, and the only source of salvation is to create (to act) in good faith. Freddy's prose may not reveal the work of a major artist, as Gardner has suggested and as Robert A. Morace has argued, but the most important factor for consideration in the manuscript he gives to Jack Winesap is not the quality of the prose but the "testing of values."[14]

13. Cowart, *Arches and Light*, 164.
14. Morace, *"Freddy's Book*, Moral Fiction, and Writing as a Mode of Thought," 206–207.

What Freddy discovers is that neither his father's expository presentation of facts nor Winesap's fabrication of them can have the same effect on the reader as a great work of art. Freddy would like his book to teach and inspire in the same way as Bernt Notke's "St. George and the Dragon." Used as a propaganda device by King Gustav, the huge wood carving is supposed to represent Sweden (Saint George) slaying all foreigners (the Dragon), a symbol of the new independent state created by Gustav's rebellion against the ruling power of Denmark. A work of art, however, as Gardner has said many times, is more than mere propaganda, though politicians, critics, and misguided artists and/or philosophers often do not understand the difference. As the reaction of Freddy's protagonist Lars-Goren reveals, Notke's work contains a power much greater than that of propaganda and a multitude of meanings:

> What he saw was the blank, staring face of the knight, gazing straight forward, motionless, as if indifferent to the monster, gazing as if mad or entranced or blind, infinitely gentle, infinitely sorrowful, beyond all human pain. I am Sweden, he seemed to say — or something more than Sweden. *I am humanity, living and dead.* For it did not seem to Lars-Goren that the monster below the belly of the violently trembling horse could be described as, simply, "foreigners," as the common interpretation maintained. It was evil itself; death, oblivion, every conceivable form of human loss.[15]

A great work of art, Freddy suggests, transcends its literal or intentional meanings and moves people to a deeper faith in themselves and others. Even more than "The Old Mill" in *The Resurrection*, "St. George and the Dragon" in Freddy's novella is suffused with the kind of artistic vision or wholeness that a person must have in order to come to an understanding of himself and the world in which he lives. Lars-Goren, like James Chandler, senses the power of such art but does not understand it until he has nearly completed his journey.

In having Freddy create Lars-Goren as an alter ego, Gardner establishes Freddy's ideal counterpart and works out his moral aim within the very basic characterization of the mythical hero that he discusses in *On Moral Fiction* and portrays through Beowulf at the end of *Grendel*: "Every hero's proper function is to provide a noble image for men to be inspired and guided by in their own actions; that is, the hero's business is to reveal what the gods require and love . . . the business of the poet . . . is to celebrate the work of the hero, pass the image on,

---

15. John Gardner, *Freddy's Book* (New York, 1980), 147. Further references to this edition will be made in the text.

keep the heroic model of behavior fresh, generation on generation."[16] As Freddy's hero, the knight Lars-Goren must make an art of his role in life, for he has no other pretensions. Like Freddy, he aims to embody or reproduce somehow the effect of the work of art he admires; he wishes to be like the knight Saint George, who has risen to a higher plane of existence akin to Gardner's "aesthetic wholeness."

Lars-Goren is also a version of Gardner's moral artist, sharing a background similar to that of the protagonists in all of Gardner's novels. Lars-Goren seems to draw "his strength in large measure from his pastoral origins," but he sacrifices the security and comfort derived from his family and his community in order to serve his country and his friend King Gustav.[17] When he returns home after Gustav has been crowned, he feels as though he has been "reborn" (123), and as if he is "a long, long way from where the Devil schemed and plotted" (130). But Lars-Goren is not at peace with himself, for he feels the usual overwhelming guilt of Gardner's protagonists. " 'I always feel guilty,' " he confesses to his wife, Liv, " 'coming through the villages when I've been away so long,' " and at " 'not being here to see the children grow up' " (127). From the first time he sees the Devil, he is seized with paralyzing fear, and once the Devil becomes an advisor to Gustav, Lars-Goren no longer is able to offer the kind of sound advice for which he is known. Eventually he admits his fears to Liv, who not surprisingly for readers familiar with Gardner's female intercessors, provides the help he is seeking. " 'I'm afraid of the Devil.' He told her what had happened, and how he'd felt an overwhelming, senseless terror." " 'Perhaps it's only rage,' she said. . . . 'Is it so terrible to feel rage for no reason?' " (153). Although Liv is developed only as the sacrificing wife who keeps house, raises the children, and soothes her knightly husband (a stereotype resulting perhaps from Freddy's lack of contact with women except in the medieval histories and fairy tales he reads), she does offer some insight into human nature. When Lars-Goren kills the Devil, he is aided by her reassurring words: " 'Yes,' he thought, 'my wife was right as usual. It was rage that made me tremble; fear that the chaos is in myself, as in everything around me' " (231).

Although the pastoral confines of Halsingland provide a retreat for Lars-Goren on two occasions in the novella and he suffers when he is separated from them, Halsingland is never portrayed as a part of an Edenic world. When Lars-Goren makes the rounds of villages on his

16. Gardner, *On Moral Fiction*, 28–29.
17. Cowart, *Arches and Light*, 153.

first trip home after Gustav's coronation, he relishes the beauty of the countryside, but he also sees the reality of a life in which old women must work the fields when sons have been killed in wars and peasants must eat bread made from tree bark when crops have failed. In addition, the peasants are revealed as gossiping, " 'empty-headed fools,' " not the solid "salt of the earth" of Romantic vision. Lars-Goren's guilt is only increased by these negative aspects of common life, for as knight of Halsingland, he is responsible for the care and education of his people. On his second trip home, accompanied by Bishop Brask, Lars-Goren's pleasant reverie with his family is undercut by the bishop's reflections on Halsingland. " 'It's one of those dreams of innocence, this place,' " Brask says, " 'It's easy enough to live justly here. What's to prevent it? But . . . the future's with cities; you know that yourself.' He gave an apologetic little shrug. 'Cities are where the wealth is, and the power that makes your little hideaway safe or not safe' " (214). And the city soon does invade Lars-Goren's retreat when a messenger arrives with the news that Brask and Lars-Goren are sought under a death edict by King Gustav because they have not followed his command to kill the Devil.

As usual, the natural world in Gardner's fiction provides some relief from the complexities of life, but those very complexities are making any hope of Eden less and less possible. In *Freddy's Book*, the Spencerian notion of evolution toward an ideal state has been supplanted by what might be called Bishop Brask's Machiavellian theory of evolution. Brask's philosophy is to survive at any cost and by any means, but he has lost sight of any reason for survival. Gardner also continues to undercut the Romantic vision of rural life by revealing the darker side of nature and its inhabitants. The witch-burning, which Lars-Goren approves of as a traditional way of life in Halsingland, is a good example. Lars-Goren is able to maintain the innocence and faith he has gained from his pastoral origins, but he also learns, with the help of Liv, Brask, and the artist Bernt Notke, that clinging blindly to tradition only leads to fear and defeat. The question becomes whether it is possible to maintain any small part of the paradise lost, even if Eden is only a testimony to the power of imagination, a state of mind like that possessed by the Lapps who are "in tune with the wind and snow, the heartbeat of the reindeer, the mind of God" (238). In spite of all of the undercutting he uses, Gardner seems to answer the question affirmatively in *Freddy's Book*. One may not be able to "be like the Lapps," as Lars-Goren's son Erik argues, but Lars-Goren does enter their world, and perhaps because of his Lapp blood and/or his faith, is able to kill the Devil, though he drags Brask, crying out for reason, with him all the way.

An Edenic existence may no longer be possible for men of reason, as Brask and Erik Bergquist believe, but the unspoiled culture of the Lapps suggests otherwise for Freddy, who seems to be saying that if one retreats far enough, farther even from society than the pastoral Halsingland, he comes to a land where nature, mind, and God are one. Although Lappland does not possess the bountiful attraction of the Old Testament paradise, it does seem to mirror Lars-Goren's indomitable spirit. " 'It's something about the simplicity,' " Lars-Goren tries to explain to his family, " 'the absolute simplicity of the landscape, the light, the inescapable concern with necessities, nothing more' " (149). Lars-Goren, after all, has Lapp blood and has also inherited "second-sight" from his Lapp kin, so he remains, in a sense, party to what the other people around him have long since lost. A sympathetic imagination, Gardner suggests, may allow us to partake of pastoral pleasures even if we cannot, as mythical heroes do, retreat physically into an Edenic world. Lappland is as much a state of mind as a geographical location, and if it does not represent the faith and innocence of human goodness that existed before the Fall, it does at least reflect the potential power of the human imagination. The Devil, as we know, resides in this paradise, but he is revealed also as only another part of human nature, another figment of the imagination.

These retreats into nature, where family and community still exist, help to move Lars-Goren toward a greater understanding of himself, and as such they become the gatherings of *Freddy's Book*. Although Bishop Brask tempers any idealistic view Lars-Goren may have of his homeland, Lars-Goren's belief that the people of Halsingland — and people everywhere, for that matter — are noble creatures is reinforced when he goes with his family to see the statue of "St. George and the Dragon": "It was as if, without the people, the statue was incomplete, unreal as a miracle in a grotto where there is no human eye to witness it. . . . Peasants, burghers, knights in fine dress stood motionless, gazing up, some of them weeping, hardly bothering to dab away the tears. Lars-Goren looked at them and felt a ringing in his heart that he could hardly put a name to, whether pain or awe or love or something else" (146–47). This gathering increases Lars-Goren's faith in humanity and leads to the realization that he cannot cling blindly to the past. Change is inevitable, as Bishop Brask constantly reminds Lars-Goren, but it is not, as Brask would have him believe, necessarily always for the worse. As he stands in the crowd surrounding the great carving, Lars-Goren suddenly knows that the witch-burning he permitted was wrong and that his son Erik was intuitively correct in opposing it. The gathering also allows Freddy to make the point that without people to be affected by it, art's only function is personal expression. Such a declaration adds to what we already know about Freddy's struggle toward personal salvation. Long before Winesap arrives at the Agaards' home, Freddy concludes that he must make contact again with the world, for without a reader other than himself, "King Gustav and the Devil" will never be more than bibliotherapy.

Until he acts to complete his mission, Lars-Goren cannot fully understand the powerful effect that his art—his life—may have on others. Forced from his retreat in Halsingland, he travels with Bishop Brask to Lappland in search of the Devil. As in *The Resurrection*, the ominous stranger of *Freddy's Book* appears first in a dream. Lars-Goren associates the old peasant woman of his dreams with the "witch" he allowed his people to burn: "He carried with him all that night, both awake and asleep, an unsettling image of the witch's face, for some reason the face of the old peasant woman. . . . She stared straight ahead of her, with an expression he could not fathom, as if she were looking at something no one else could see" (140). The threatening messenger appears in person (as a ghost) when Lars-Goren and Brask are about to cross into Lappland, and she reveals that the source of Lars-Goren's guilt and fear is his own human frailty:

> "If I am damned, then you are ten thousand times damned, Lars-Goren. You are called a great fighter and a wise counselor, and you are praised as a man who is afraid of nothing in the world except the Devil. But I have come to tell you you are a coward and a fool, for you shiver at a Nothing—mere stench and black air, for that is what he is, your wide-winged Devil—and in the presence of the greatest evil ever dreamt of, the fact that we exist in the world at all, helpless as babes against both evil and seeming good, you do not have the wit to blanch at all." (226)

Although Bishop Brask condemns the witch for attacking Lars-Goren's character, which he has come to admire, Lars-Goren understands that " 'she's right, and you're right. We all are. . . . It's right to cry out for justice beyond anything else. If *we* can dream of justice, surely *God* can too' " (230). Just as courage, love, and faith should not be scoffed at or denied, fear, guilt, and rage should not be suppressed, for all are parts of human nature. Gardner's emphasis is on feelings, and all feelings, as well as experiences, are valuable in the search for meaning. One great difference between the knight and the bishop is that Lars-Goren allows himself to be guided on occasion by his feelings, whereas Brask has suppressed all feelings in favor of rhetoric. Nevertheless, just as Henry Soames in *Nickel Mountain* needs the example of George Loomis' failure to overcome his despair and guilt, Lars-Goren needs Bishop Brask's rhetoric and sacrifice to defeat the Devil.

As with other failed artists in Gardner's novels, Bishop Brask is developed sympathetically in *Freddy's Book*. A critical yet well-rounded portrait of Brask, who may be based on William Gass, is in keeping with Freddy's novella as well, since Freddy's Brask no doubt originates with Professor Agaard, as Gardner himself has suggested.[18] The two men are similar in age and disposition, and they both suffer from doubts about themselves and the value of their lives. Bishop Brask defends the Church against all politicians as stubbornly as Sven Agaard defends the traditional approach to history against brash innovators like Jack Winesap, although Freddy instills in Brask a more philosophical turn of mind than Professor Agaard possesses. Freddy's father seems a reincarnation of the crotchety James Page, bent on defending absolutes that may no longer be of value in the modern world, whereas Brask is closer to Gardner's philosophical protagonists James Chandler and Peter Mickelsson, who suffer from the illusion that reason alone can lead to understanding.

Although Brask has also been compared to "Gardner's anarchists," the bishop is not just a clone of a previous creation of Gardner's nor is he beyond "conversion," as are Agathon, Taggert Hodge, and Grendel. Unlike the monk of "The Temptation of St. Ivo" who violates his vows to help a fellow human being and to save the mythical Phoenix (a symbol of the regeneration achieved by art), Freddy's bishop is a man who has carefully examined life and found nothing of value but rhetoric and style. Brask may appear to be more of a Jack Winesap than a Sven Agaard in this respect, having discovered that a clever gesture or a carefully turned phrase has a more persuasive effect on people than mere facts, but Winesap does say of Agaard, "Angry as he made me, I had to give the old man an A for rhetoric" (34). Brask's problem, however, is more complex than either Agaard's or Winesap's, for Brask believes in nothing. Having developed his reasoning powers to such an extent that he can view both sides of an issue equally well, Brask's only concern be-

18. Winther, "An Interview with John Gardner," 521.

comes his own survival. Often mere stasis allows him to avoid becoming involved in political intrigues that might cost him his power or his life. Such stasis, for Gardner, is one of the worst sins, and nowhere in Gardner's fiction is a character more paralyzed than the bishop in Freddy's novella. Like the artist who stares into the abyss and concludes that nothing matters in such a chaotic world, Brask clings desperately to language itself in order to avoid being swallowed up by the nothingness that may await us all. Brask has become a master rhetorician, but like those writers who Gardner believes are lesser artists, Brask uses his well-developed skill to no particular end except his own amusement. He is, in fact, very much like the Devil: "Dry as a spider, the old bishop listened to the desiccate kiss of his rhetoric, the grotesquely chiming rhymes: *conviction, revulsion, emotion, objection.* How was he to feel anything worthy of even the debased coin 'feeling,' he asked himself, limited forever to the predictable trapezoids of his mind's drab spiderweb, language?" (169). As Gardner says in one interview, "absolutely rigorous argument can lead to mutually exclusive positions," and eventually one must go on to "a different basis of knowledge."[19] For Gardner, the different basis of knowledge is "honest feeling," but Bishop Brask has so suppressed his feelings that he is unable to see that he still has an alternative to the mutually exclusive, and equally depressing, views derived through logic: "What did it matter what he thought, after all? Life would go on, or would go on until it stopped" (181).

Like James Page in *October Light,* Bishop Brask is unwillingly drawn from his isolation by the presence of a Beatrice figure. The saintly intercessors in Gardner's fiction are usually females, but Gardner's hints at Brask's homosexuality—his mincing walk (111), his love for another man (208)—make it only fitting that Lars-Goren effectively intercedes in Brask's life in the same way Liv, Lars-Goren's wife, guides her husband toward the insight that enables him to deal with his fear and guilt. Lars-Goren does not so much enter into debates with Brask as afford a model of virtue and faith that Brask tries to soil with his empty rhetoric and existential philosophy. Brask becomes a much greater temptor for Lars-Goren than the Devil does because he represents the temper of modern times that Lars-Goren soon releases by "killing superstition and myth." Brask's arguments are effective in stimulating Lars-Goren to question and evaluate his life, but Lars-Goren intuitively knows that Brask is wrong. Professor Agaard's rhet-

19. Harvey, "Where Philosophy and Fiction Meet," 74.

oric similarly affects Freddy's art, but does little to change the giant's view of the world.

Somewhat ironically, Brask and Professor Agaard are more profoundly influenced by Lars-Goren and Freddy than vice versa. Just as James Page is shocked by the realization that he still has the power to love, a power stirred in him by the presence of his old friend Estelle Parks, so Bishop Brask is surprised to think "that Lars-Goren might somehow, by his stubborn innocence, 'save Brask's soul' " (220). Lars-Goren's presence also causes Brask to remember the love he once felt for another human being and, in effect, for God (208). In a similar manner, Freddy's development as an artist, which we can see in the gradual improvement of style, thematic emphasis, and character development in "King Gustav and the Devil," has had an effect on his father. Although Sven Agaard has not read Freddy's book, he knows Freddy's preferences in literature and philosophy, and, as he confesses, one of the reasons he invites Winesap to visit is because Freddy has " 'read [Winesap's] books. . . . He's a kind of fan' " (43). Professor Agaard's need to confront Winesap reveals some doubt in Agaard's mind about the validity of his own beliefs, but, like Brask, he argues his case so vehemently that his opponent scarcely has a chance to reply.

Bishop Brask and Professor Agaard are never able to "unlock" their hearts and admit they have been wrong, as their counterpart James Page does in *October Light*. Agaard is convinced he has won the debate with Winesap even though we hear in his final words, " 'You win, Professor. I agree' " (59), a certain resignation to all the Winesaps, with their unquestioning reliance on psychoanalysis, who have come to supplant him and set Freddy free. In his novella, Freddy moves his father-figure, Brask, toward the kind of conversion he probably wishes his own father could undergo. The closer Brask gets to the Devil, the more he spouts his rhetoric but the less effect it has. In fact, Brask begins to get a little euphoric at the possibility that he and Lars-Goren may accomplish their mission. Just making the decision to act on something causes him to think " 'this is poetry, this is love and religion!' " (242). His inability to give up his rhetoric serves a useful purpose, however, in distracting the Devil so Lars-Goren can slit his throat.

The love of language, which Brask and the Devil share, results in their deaths. Brask's sacrifice, like those of other failed artists in Gardner's novels, allows the protagonist to achieve the level of understanding he has been seeking. Language is powerful, Gardner suggests, but language alone cannot sustain life, and language alone cannot make a work of art great. But Brask's involvement in killing the Devil also suggests that neither can perfect intuition and faith create great art without language to pass on those values through the "art of fiction."

In the same way that Freddy incorporates much of his father's nature into the character of Bishop Brask, he also uses what knowledge he has of Jack Winesap to flesh out his version of King Gustav. Although Freddy does not meet Winesap until after "King Gustav and the Devil" is completed, he is familiar enough with Winesap's theories to have some sense of the man, and he has obviously imitated the psychohistorian's techniques of "fabulation" in writing his novella.[20] Gustav is a historical figure who is described in the books Freddy has studied, but it seems to me that in developing the fictional Gustav, Gardner uses and then transcends Freddy's knowledge of the Swedish king and of Winesap in order to strengthen the similarities of the two characters. Winesap and Gustav, for instance, make a pretense of modesty despite the obvious striking effects they have on the audiences they address. Under attack, however, they find their self-depreciating acts eroding and react with fear and anger. Professor Agaard and Freddy, and the conditions under which they live, shake Winesap from his comfortable life and reawaken him to the bitterness and cruelty that exist in the world outside of academic debates and imaginative speculations about the past. Similarly, Bishop Brask and Lars-Goren remind Gustav that his vision of an ideal political state is crumbling under the reality of everyday conditions in Sweden.

In fact, all of the characters in *Freddy's Book* have a tendency to classify people and create systems of order, and all have their classification systems upset. Winesap, for instance, is completely puzzled by Agaard's manner and actions; Lars-Goren does not fit into Brask's system of observation; Freddy confounds both his father and Winesap. Just as Gustav believes that the death of the Devil (along with the deaths of Brask and Lars-Goren) might possibly "save" his vision of a powerful, democratic Sweden, so Winesap believes that medical science might help Freddy. Obviously, Gardner suggests, these answers are too easy; something more is needed to set people on the right path toward healthier, freer, and more productive lives. The first step toward "enlightenment" might be the killing of the Devil, since Gardner seems to equate the beginnings of the Renaissance with the beginnings of the modern age as

20. Morace, *"Freddy's Book*, Moral Fiction, and Writing as a Mode of Thought," 211.

we know it, and the first step for Freddy's rehabilitation might be medical and/or psychiatric help, as Winesap recommends to Professor Agaard. But eventually the movement toward true salvation, redemption, and reintegration requires more than physical action; it requires the innocent faith and love of Lars-Goren, a touch of which Winesap finally displays by exchanging manuscripts with Freddy. Winesap moves from self-confidence to anger and frustration at Agaard and himself, to horror at Freddy's physical condition, to fear of Freddy. In a similar manner, Gustav moves from self-confidence to anger at his political opponents, to frustration with his own leadership, to fear of his allies—the Devil, Brask, and Lars-Goren. With the death of the Devil, the sacrifice of Brask, and the heroism of Lars-Goren, Gustav's anger and fear are suddenly dispelled and he vows to let the people decide the fate of Sweden. When Freddy offers his book to Winesap, Winesap, too, loses his fear and projects his lifted spirit onto Freddy: "[Freddy] seemed to move more lightly now, as if it had been a great weight he'd carried, that gift he'd brought" (64). To speculate on what happens to Winesap after he reads "King Gustav and the Devil" is fruitless, although to my way of thinking, if Freddy's moral fiction is as effective as Gardner's, Winesap, like the rest of us, will be changed at least in some small way for having had his encounter with Freddy and his creations. That a weight seems lifted from the both of them in *Freddy's Book* suggests such a change.

Although some critics have taken the final lines of "King Gustav and the Devil" (in fact the final lines of *Freddy's Book*) to be a pessimistic vision of the modern age, I believe they have overlooked Gardner's actual intent. Compare Freddy's final lines with the final lines of Wallace Stevens' "Sunday Morning":

> And now, like wings spreading, darkness fell. There was no light anywhere, except for the yellow light of cities. (246)

> > And, in the isolation of the sky,
> > At evening, casual flocks of pigeons make
> > Ambiguous undulations as they sink,
> > Downward to darkness, on extended wings.[21]

The shared images of wings spreading darkness over the earth are important, I think, especially if we remember that Gardner has drawn on Stevens before. In *The Resurrection*, the lines from "Connoisseur of Chaos" offer the reconciled vision for which James Chandler has been

---

21. Wallace Stevens, "Sunday Morning," in *Collected Poems of Wallace Stevens* (New York, 1982), 70.

desperately searching. And in *On Moral Fiction*, as he presents a brief history of moral art, Gardner says that in "Peter Quince at the Clavier" Stevens suggests "God still exists . . . but we've swallowed him."[22] Certainly, both of these ideas are at the center of *Freddy's Book*, and if we recall that the reconciling line of "Sunday Morning" — "Death is the mother of beauty" — seems to answer questions about reality and existence raised by Stevens in his poetry written before "Sunday Morning," then Freddy's final lines are not despairing. I also think that critics who see bleakness in Freddy's lines because the only light comes from the cities have taken Bishop Brask's view rather than Freddy's or Gardner's. It is Brask who condemns the cities as bastions of corruption and nihilism, who cries out facetiously and with the same blindness as the lawyer in Melville's "Bartleby the Scrivener": " 'Ah yes, poor humanity! Poor Sweden!' " (216). Gardner might appear to agree with Brask's appraisal, since he does use the urban/rural contrast a great deal in his novels, but Gardner understands, as Brask does not, that corruption and nihilism come not from any external source — no more from cities than from the Devil — but from within human beings. The lights at the end of "King Gustav and the Devil" are lights of hope, not despair, for in the cities live the people who are going to determine the fate of Gustav's democracy, and all people contain the potential for good as well as for evil.

The real monster in *Freddy's Book* is not Gustav's horned trickster but Brask's boredom with life and distaste for humanity (168). For this reason, I have not dealt with the Devil as a character in *Freddy's Book*. He seems to work less as a character than as a set of values that cannot be changed or as a creation of our imaginations for which we have no explanation. Whereas at the center of the triangle of Winesap, Freddy, and Agaard exists the question of how to deal with history, at the center of the triangle of Gustav, Lars-Goren, and Bishop Brask rests the question of how to deal with the Devil. Freddy internalizes his father's historical facts and uses Winesap's imaginative reconstruction to create a work of art whose effect is more powerful than facts or fabrication alone, and Lars-Goren internalizes the Devil in all of his guises — witch, bishop, politician — to create a different kind of life, if not better, at least more truthful than his previous one. Lars-Goren, like Freddy, acts to achieve a rewarding aesthetic vision, in effect making life art.

22. Gardner, *On Moral Fiction*, 37.

With *Freddy's Book*, Gardner seems to be moving away from the carefully detailed "resurrections" of his previous novels. The oddness of *Freddy's Book* might be explained by Freddy's lack of control as a writer, except that Freddy has nothing to do with the tale of Jack Winesap. Perhaps Gardner is merely reacting to the increasing amount of criticism, both positive and negative, which uses *On Moral Fiction* as a touchstone to all his work, by consciously making his work more obscure. Resolution is apparent in *Freddy's Book*, but it is much more subtly revealed. As we have seen, *Mickelsson's Ghosts* also leaves the reader somewhat unsure of the protagonist's reintegration and raises questions about a new direction in Gardner's fiction that may remain unanswered.

5

Posthumous Novels
Stillness
and *Shadows*

"Process is all I care about."
—MARTIN ORRICK in *Shadows*

Stillness

John Gardner's imaginative account of his first marriage is the basis for the autobiographical novel *Stillness*. Unlike *Shadows, Stillness* exists in a completed draft, but Gardner abandoned it, and one can only guess at how his usually extensive revision methods would have expanded the rather straightforward and hurriedly written narrative. Certainly the two stories, "Stillness" and "Redemption," which he extracted from *Stillness*, are greatly altered.[1] *Stillness*, in fact, is more characteristic of Gardner's short stories than of his novels. It is the only novel with artists, the novelist Martin and the musician Joan Orrick, as protagonists (unless one counts Freddy Agaard), and although the Orricks, who are also cousins, have spent most of their lives together, the reintegrations they undergo seem a little forced, an indication that Gardner had decided on the pattern he wanted the novel to take but had not yet enlarged the Orricks' rediscovery of themselves. I get the impression that not only are these two characters, who cannot live without one another, desperate to ease the tensions of their relationship but also that Gardner was straining to show with the Orricks how the problems of his own marriage could be resolved through art. Although Gardner gave up on the novel several years before his mar-

---

1. John Gardner, *The Art of Living and Other Stories* (New York, 1981), 30–64.

riage to Joan Patterson ended in divorce, *Stillness* is the most intensely personal and moving attempt by Gardner to make life art.

Other than the gossip such a novel might generate (Gardner and his wife Joan supposedly transcribed much of it from conversations recorded as "an exercise of recall"), *Stillness* is interesting because of its unrevised skeletal starkness, and also because it is the only novel in which a woman, Joan Orrick, appears to upstage the male protagonist and become the moral artist who succeeds in changing her life and the lives of those around her.[2]

In the Prologue to *Stillness*, we are told it would be "useless, as always, to inquire too narrowly [or 'too earnestly'] what Martin Orrick meant" by certain passages in his novels that focus on nature and metaphysics (4, 13). These, of course, are territories Gardner staked out for his own fiction: the natural world in which we originated but from which we have through some quirk of evolution been separated, and the intellectual world we have developed to make sense somehow of our uniqueness (or mutancy). Garner's warning about Martin Orrick's fiction suggests that if a work of art is to survive the passage of time, it will thwart attempts to explain all of its effects in rational terms. Additionally, it seems to me, Gardner is warning us that the story he is about to tell in *Stillness* will reveal more about Martin's life and beliefs than the passages on nature and metaphysics quoted from Martin's books. And finally, the warning says, *Stillness* may not be as much Martin's story, since he escapes into his fiction in order to work out the problems of his life, as it is Joan's, for once she gives up her musical career for Martin and her children, she is faced daily with the problem of defining her role in life.

As most of the Orricks' friends view them, Martin is the novelist, Joan the novelist's wife. The sacrificial nature of Joan's life is revealed in the first few pages of the novel when she suffers an attack of an as-yet undefined illness and is carried to the car to be taken to the hospital: "She hung limp between them, like the figure of Christ in some descent from the cross" (11). Although Joan was a musical prodigy and has been a concert pianist, no one thinks of her as an artist after her marriage to Martin, and eventually she comes to see herself as inseparable from him: "But it would come to her, finally, what it was that made her cling to him. . . . He was her past, her whole life, and if he left her . . . her whole life would be cancelled, made meaningless" (22–23).

2. John Gardner, *Stillness and Shadows*, ed. with introduction by Nicholas Delbanco (New York, 1986), xiii. Further references to this edition will be made in the text.

By devoting nearly half of the novel to detailed descriptions of the personalities and lives of parents, grandparents, aunts, and uncles, Gardner emphasizes the importance of Joan and Martin's shared past. The Orricks are locked together yet haunted by their past, and in a sense it is the source of their problems because their relatives, through different combinations of the same genes, have produced two people not only of opposite sexes but also of opposite natures. To represent the basis of the Orricks' relationship, Gardner develops an image of the "split-brain." In so far as Martin is the left lobe or intellect and Joan is the right lobe or intuition, the Orricks are bound together physically but perceive the world in entirely different ways.

Even in the perception of their shared families, Joan and Martin cannot agree. The ghosts of the past — their own pasts and that of their families — contain knowledge for them, but the knowledge only confirms what we already know of their differences. Whereas Martin remembers Grandma Davis for "her reading of the story of Samuel," Joan recalls nothing extraordinary about the old woman's religious opinions. "Perhaps," Martin thinks, "[Joan had] seen past Grandma Davis's opinions instinctively" (52). As in *Nickel Mountain* and *Mickelsson's Ghosts*, ominous strangers surround the protagonists in *Stillness,* but their messages go unnoticed or are misinterpreted. Yet the "genetic connection" between Joan and Martin must contain some point of intersection, just as the human brain's left and right lobes are connected and communicate with one another.

The randomness and intense ordering of the natural world are also represented within the lives of the two protagonists of *Stillness.* Martin is "a dark one," as Joan's mother describes him. Withdrawn, sensitive, eventually suicidal, he is Gardner's intellectual artist, and his life parallels the retreat, internal evaluation, and reemergence of Gardner's protagonists. In Martin's life, however, we have not just one cycle but a series of them. Descended from an "old family" of western New York state, Martin has inherited the customs and habits of a long line of Republican, Presbyterian preachers, country lawyers, and schoolmasters. When Joan and Martin first meet as children, she recognizes immediately his "strange nature" (26), for Joan, whose family is from Missouri, represents the brightness, warmth, humor, and openness of the Midwest (27). As she draws him from the narrowness of his eastern upbringing, she comes to embody "a special aliveness" for him: "He was in love with her. . . . In love with her whole family, her world," and "despite the odd care she took of him, he had no idea that she was also in love with him" (27). She makes him happy, and her world, the Midwest, "always had for him, and would have all his life, a 'vast benevolent electric charge, a smell of the miraculous' " (27). The first cycle in Martin's life ends when he discovers his love for Joan and her world.

A second cycle begins when Martin, at the age of seven, kills his brother Gilbert in a farm accident. He experiences, at this early age, the guilt and despair that most of Gardner's protagonists accumulate over a lifetime. He is drawn gradually from this "dark wood" by music and by the old musician Yegudkin. Like Jack Hawthorne in the short story "Redemption," Martin is able to reenter the world of the living only through the saving grace of art. Oddly enough, Joan, though she is a wonderful musician, plays little part in Martin's salvation, as if Gardner wants to make clear that she is not to be one of his female intercessors but has a story of her own to tell.

The third cycle, and the most important one in *Stillness*, occurs during the period of Martin's marriage to Joan. By the time they are established in San Francisco where Martin is teaching, he has "no faith" in himself or in life generally. His despair has become a metaphysical problem, and he tries to work out solutions in the "gloomy" novels he writes. Martin becomes convinced that Joan is out to destroy him. He finds her "needs" repulsive, and he agrees with her accusation that he does not need a "fucking living soul" (22).

Martin's paranoia and coldness "terrify" Joan. Unlike her husband and cousin, Joan has always been outgoing and self-confident. Men are attracted by her beauty and wit, and because she was a prodigy, she never understands the relentlessness with which Martin must pursue his own art in order for it to succeed. She leads him through life, protects him, and prevents him from growing up, thus insuring his dependence on her. She is uninterested in ideas, philosophy, or artistic theory, and she cannot understand Martin's need to search for answers and to live in a world of abstractions. Neither can she understand his attraction to the oppressing atmosphere of her native region, the Ozarks, for she prefers the society and liveliness of the city.

The extreme differences between Joan and Martin prevent them from communicating with one another. Language itself fails them. Joan hides behind caustic humor and tears, and Martin withdraws into his own world of alcohol and art. When they try to talk, the words they speak are never interpreted correctly. Martin, for instance, sees Joan's "need" for him as a weakness, and despite the prodigious memory that Martin displays in his fiction, Joan believes he has "for-gotten" how much they once loved one another. Martin has not for-gotten their love, but he has become convinced that it was an illusion.

Even on the common ground of art, where we might expect them to find some comfort in one another, some sense of relief from the con-stant conflict of wills, they turn out to be creating in different ways and from different sources. Joan is intuitive and has great power of imagi-nation. Her musical talent arises from a feeling for her instrument, from the "right lobe of the brain," and she senses at the center of art a "stillness" that momentarily holds off the slipping of the world into darkness. Like Henry Soames and James Page, she is filled with feel-ing but inarticulate (121). Martin is rational and makes up for a lack of imagination by exploring ideas that he transposes into characters and situations in his novels. His art evolves from this relentless testing of ideas in an attempt to discover some stability and to convince him-self that life is more than "an accidental tumble of the dice." Although he hates idealists, he wonders if "one could learn . . . to enjoy the bangings, celebrate the swiftly passing patterns as holy." He writes not to discover a "stillness"—a moment that holds off change—but to "make the beauty of change everlasting" (12–13). While Joan is inclined to accept change (as long as it does not interfere with her marriage) and death, Martin is relentless in his attempt to solve the mystery of mutability.

Joan is willing to try to improve their relationship, but Martin re-fuses to accept the idea that any alteration in their lives is possible. Even as he denies the strength of individual will, however, he won-ders, "why *shouldn't* a man's life develop reasonably, like a plot, with choices along the way, and antagonists with names, and some grand, compelling purpose, and a ringing final line?" (74). But he has no more faith in his ability to alter his own life than he does in the power of his art to discover truth. The attempt to make life art is doomed, Martin believes, for art and nature have no connection: "Nature's love stories had nothing to do with those novelists make up; nature's sus-pense has no meaning beyond the obvious, that that which is mind-lessly, inexorably coming has, for better or worse, not yet arrived" (74). Life appears determined, by genes or by the stars or by fate, and it moves surely toward entropy. What happens in between is not a matter of choice, Martin Orrick believes, but of chance. Unable to act, Martin stagnates within himself and within his marriage to Joan.

Withdrawn into their separate worlds, Joan and Martin cannot see themselves or one another clearly until they encounter a succession of intercessors. While Martin is on a visiting professorship at the University of Detroit, he and Joan meet Paul Brotsky, one of Gardner's failed artists. A survivor of the Vietnam War, Paul has "the necessary sympathy born of pain, the necessary intelligence and insight, even wisdom, and more than the necessary ability with words" to be a great fiction writer, "but grief and self-doubt made his heart unsteady, undermined his purpose" (67–68). Paul's ability to empathize with both Joan and Martin, however, becomes very valuable: "Paul understood and partly sympathized with [Joan's] indifference to the ultimate truth Martin Orrick had no faith in but was forever in quest of" (71). What Martin cannot do for Joan, Paul Brotsky does "easily and with pleasure — repairs around the house, shopping errands, above all, talk with Joan" (70). He is also able to draw Martin out and discuss intelligently those theories of "time, or split-brain psychology, or Baxter's psychic plants" (70). With Martin's unspoken approval, Paul often meets Joan to make love (another of her needs Martin fails to fulfill), and the three become so close that they sometimes even sleep together. Paul provides mental and physical stability for the Orricks' marriage. He is the common ground on which Joan and Martin can meet, and his important message to the both of them is that people can "change their lives."

If Paul Brotsky is not the Orricks' deliverer, he is at least Joan's saintly intercessor. He enters the Orricks' lives at a critical time, for they meet soon after Martin has taken his family back to the Midwest to live and after Joan learns from Martin's psychiatrist that Martin cannot love her as he once did. " 'To your husband you are a symbol of evil and repression. He may grow out of this, though the odds are not good. He may well become an artist of some stature, and he may become a healthy and confident man, but his attitude toward you . . . ' " (134). The psychiatrist trails off, leaving unspoken the dark possibilities. To save herself and her children, Joan concludes, she must divorce Martin, but somehow this rational conclusion is less powerful than her love for her husband and family. When she also falls in love with Paul Brotsky, his ability to meditate between her and Martin solidifies her feeling that she and Martin can save themselves and their marriage: "She began to believe something was changing, it would perhaps be all right" (135).

Although Martin takes Joan and the children with him to Missouri, his decision to leave San Francisco is a flight of desperation "to the only solid truth he could remember." He abandons himself to nature, "to a place—a set of emotions, principles, if you like, translated into the solidity of red earth, low, angry mountains, huge, slow-moving rivers, cyclones, birds and snakes" (136). As with most of Gardner's protagonists, Martin discovers something of himself in the retreat. He cannot remain immersed in this natural world and must emerge again into the world from which he has retreated, but "the woman who would awaken him to the truth about his wife was inevitable there, and he would find there, also, the Ferndeans, who would recall him to himself" (136). Martin's flight is an action of spontaneity and self-assertion, and he is rewarded for breaking free of his passivity.

For Martin, the Midwest represents the pastoral world that Gardner evokes again and again in his fiction. To make his life whole, Martin needs such a place. He discovers Joan in the Midwest, he attends college in the Midwest, and he returns to the Midwest after his period of insanity in San Francisco. Despite its "ticks, chiggers, and copperheads, rattlesnakes and cottonmouths, cyclones and devastating floods," the Midwest is a "moral center" for Martin and the place where he finally decides to take control of his life (27).

Removed from the urban world she loves, Joan holds onto her marriage but sacrifices her own active life and desires in order to follow Martin into the " 'wasted heart of the country' " (136). Like several of Gardner's moral artists, Joan suffers from a specific physical ailment that threatens to shorten her life. Doctors are baffled by her bouts of pain, and when she moves back to the Midwest with Martin, she spends much of her time bedridden and unable to concentrate enough to compose music or to write, which only adds to her depression. Ironically, Joan also discovers something about herself in the Midwest. After a battery of hospital tests by specialists and even a suggestion that her problem may be psychological, the nature of her illness is finally discovered by a local Missouri general practitioner. If human beings are mutants, separated from the natural world by some chance combination of genetic material, then Joan is a mutant among mutants. Her pain, she is told, is caused by a genetic abnormality that allows adhesions (scar tissue) to grow throughout her body. There is no cure, and the only treatment is periodic surgery to remove the constrictive tissues (129). Once she understands why she hurts, Joan is able to deal with the pain. Through her example, Gardner suggests, she and Martin may be able to deal with the pain they cause one another if they can come to understand and accept themselves.

Both Joan and Martin appear to be aided in their attempts to recover some semblance of order in their lives by the Ferndeans, who have also been drawn to the Midwest by its beautiful yet threatening landscape. If Gardner had expanded *Stillness*, he would probably have given much more attention to John and Nadine Ferndean. Based on Gardner's close friendship with the sculptor Nicholas Vergette, who died of cancer in 1974, Martin's friendship with John Ferndean appears to be very intense, but Gardner does not develop Ferndean's character enough for us to understand why he has such a profound effect on Martin. Certainly Ferndean is not at all like the moody and tempestuous Martin Orrick, yet "Martin and the sculptor talked earnestly, boomingly, of the principles of art, told jokes, played loud games, fiercely argued politics or education or religion, always both of them on the same side. The world grew warmer, healthier, it seemed to Martin—became, mysteriously, more beautiful" (137).

We also never see anything of Ferndean's art. In Gardner's "John Napper Sailing Through the Universe," the protagonist is intrigued by the enthusiasm for life expressed by the artist John Napper, but he discovers in viewing Napper's paintings that Napper has used art to work through his despair and arrive at a celebration of life. In *Stillness*, we are told only that Ferndean "was also a truly extraordinary sculptor, teacher, husband and, perhaps above all, father. . . . He was no more than Martin a man bound by trivial rules. If his life was stable, conventional, 'moral' (to use a word Martin Orrick describes in one of his novels as 'obscene and despicable'), it was all those things by his free and conscious choice. In the life of John Ferndean, to put the matter briefly, Martin Orrick found rules he could approve of" (137). What these rules are or how Ferndean may have arrived at them through his art, however, we are never told.

Ferndean, his wife Nadine, and their child nevertheless have a healing effect on Martin, Joan, and their two children. They explore the Missouri landscape, take trips to Mexico and Europe, and all become "quite literally and quite perceptibly, more handsome." Joan even learns "with some amazement, how beautiful the countryside was" and falls "in love with Martin's mountains" (137–38). In addition, the Orricks' relationship improves because of Martin's success. "He'd had, by this time, three best-sellers," and he is willing to allow Joan some relief from the confinement of the Ozarks by using the money for family trips to Geneva, Paris, and England. Yet the blossoming of Joan's life is a result of more than financial security, for even when her pain returns, she continues to believe "that the world had grown healthy, buzzingly alive, charged with that deep, jungle-rich Midwestern light she'd known in her childhood" (138).

If Gardner has imbued *Stillness* with any of the sense of community that is so important in his novels, it arises from this period in the Orricks' marriage, when the Orricks, the Ferndeans, and Paul Brotsky are, for about three or four years, happy. Martin knows the peacefulness cannot last, but he is pleased that perhaps "his work, his passions, his sickness had made all this possible, and it was good, supremely beautiful" (141). Although he celebrates with his friends and family, Martin still feels "tragically separate, cut off" (141), and the loss for which he has been waiting arrives in the form of John Ferndean's incurable lung cancer. Witnessing day-by-day his once-vigorous friend's slow death is "ghastly," but "the worst of it is" that Martin falls in love with Sarah Fenton during this time and cannot keep his love secret from Joan.

Like Estelle Parks in *October Light*, Sarah Fenton is a woman of the world. Although she is only thirty-five, she has been a teacher, an actress, a practitioner of yoga, a translator at the United Nations, a traveler with gypsies, and a musician. Martin's attraction to her may be partly a result of this broad range of experience, but more likely he finds her estrangement from the rest of society—Gardner's despised and beloved "herd"—similar to his own self-imposed isolation. Like Martin, she "had no faith in herself," and "she had no code, no beliefs, or at any rate none she had words for" (151). Despite all she has done for other people, "having lived so much of her life with untouchables, God's children in India, gypsies in Spain, Mexicans, American Indians and blacks," "she'd found nothing yet to give absolute commitment to" (151). A practitioner and teacher of "Tibetan sexual exercises aimed at spiritual transcendence," a macrobiotic cook, and an "artist" of the bedroom pallet, Sarah Fenton heals Martin's bad stomach and sexual impotence. "She massaged him, taught him Do-in, convinced him that he was magnificent, drunk or sober, happy or sad" (147). She reinstills his confidence and eases his fear of women.

Unfortunately, Sarah makes Martin into the object of commitment for which she has been searching, but as much as she loves him, she is no match for Joan in the battle to win Martin's loyalty. Sarah's humility and plainness increase Martin's discomfort when he compares her with the charismatic and beautiful Joan. Sarah is somewhat vampirish —"small and thin," with "larger mournful eyes, straight, lively hair (it was black as coal), and the dry, pale mouth of someone who has lost blood" (150). Moreover, the spiritualism denoted by her appearance and interests might eventually prove more repellant than attractive to a nonbeliever like Martin. Martin is sick of the way Joan has "ruled him" and "led him around" all of his life, but when she threatens to commit suicide if he leaves her, he has no choice but to stay. Joan, Martin understands, is so much a part of him that her death would mean his own as well.

Having reached a point "beyond shame" in her attempt to hold onto Martin, Joan begins to act. She flies to her psychiatrist, Dr. Behan, in Detroit and asks him " 'to help me change myself so that Martin will love me' " (155). Behan counters, " 'You really believe, Joan, that if you get rid of certain . . . faults . . . he'll suddenly love you again as, you say, he used to?' " But Joan cannot be reasoned with, and in the presence of Paul Brotsky she is reminded that " 'people can change, save themselves' " (156–57). With her visits to Behan, Joan does begin to change. Instead of lashing out, she learns to observe, to do some of the "quiet looking and listening" of Gardner's successful artists, and she discovers that people she once would have scornfully dismissed are "more mysterious and exciting" than she had ever imagined. Instead of flaunting her own musical talents before her family, she learns to praise their amateurism and enter into their expressions of musical feeling. She even learns to cook the healthy foods Martin believes Sarah Fenton used to heal his "poisoned" body. And finally, she confronts Sarah to ask for advice on how to please Martin sexually. Joan never learns Sarah's "techniques," but she does gain Sarah's promise to break off the relationship with Martin, and she learns "how to keep from hurting him, how to show the love that had made her cling to their life" (163).

From the Missouri wilderness, Joan emerges "reborn," and her happiness at having saved her marriage fills her with a self-assertive optimism: "She *liked* herself, and the whole world loved her, and they had better keep it up or by God there was going to be hell to pay" (166). Another indication of Joan's reintegration is that she begins to consider some of the philosophical explanations of life upon which Martin broods. "Though brilliant, Joan Orrick was not a woman who often had ideas," but she begins to think that complementarity might be an answer to her problems. To describe the relationship between herself and her family, she develops an analogy of the give and take between a concert pianist and her audience. Although the pianist recognizes her artistic superiority to the audience, she needs their approval or her art is worth little more than personal satisfaction. At the same time, her art demands their attention because she plays not only for herself but also for them. In the way that Gardner's moral artist creates for himself and for an audience who he hopes will be bettered somehow by having encountered his art, Joan develops a symbiotic relationship with her family and with the community. Only through such a relationship, she realizes, will she discover in life any sense of the "stillness" that exists for her in art. Joan's final action is to undergo hypnosis in order to deal with the recurring bouts of pain caused by her illness.

When Martin is offered a teaching position at Bennington College, the Orricks for perhaps the first time are able to reach a mutually satisfactory decision. By moving to Vermont, Joan gains the social and artistic life of the East and Martin retains the small-town and rural life that he needs. The overall change in Joan's personality makes Martin "almost cheerful." Although he still complains and drives himself relentlessly with his writing and teaching and reading, his fiction begins to show something of that celebration of life he once doubted was possible.

Stillness comes to a close with Joan and Martin's marriage, if not remade, at least "settled." And yet there is something pathological about Joan Orrick's desperate actions to save her marriage. The cruelty of her confrontation with Sarah Fenton, for instance, lessens the uplifting impact of her reintegration. Martin, on the other hand, appears to dissolve into a successful career, as if Joan's change has had some magical effect on him. He becomes fat and "almost cheerful" under Joan's care. Joan may be the moral artist of *Stillness*, but there is more than a little sexism in Gardner's suggestion that all she needs to do to save her marriage is learn how to satisfy her husband's needs. Although Gardner tried in many ways to give balance to his fictional characterizations of women, he knew that endowing them with the powers of the "saintly intercessor" included the use of many traditional feminine stereotypes. As his notes indicate, he hoped to develop the female characters in *Shadows*, and in the novels to follow, as fully as the males. In *Stillness*, he had an excellent chance to do so much earlier in his career, but perhaps the personal nature of his subject matter and the failure rather than the resurrection of his own marriage prevented him from following through with the character of Joan Orrick.

Shadows

John Gardner once predicted that *Shadows*, a novel about which he had talked and on which he had worked since at least 1974, would "be either the most pompous stupid thing in the world or it [would] be a mindbreaker." From the text that novelist Nicholas Delbanco, Gardner's literary executor and editor of *Stillness and Shadows*, has chosen to publish, little can be determined about how successful the final version of the novel may have been. What we have is Book I, consisting of four chapters; Book II, consisting of five chapters; and seven fragments, all of which Delbanco chose because of their "coherence." Clearly Gardner was far from finished, although shortly before his death he is said to have told his fiancée Susan Thornton that he had finally figured out a way to "fix *Shadows*." As Delbanco points out in his introduction, not a single page of this published text or of the hundreds of other extant manuscript pages appears "unalterable as a rock," especially when compared with the complete, though unrevised and unexpanded, draft of *Stillness*. The numerous variants of certain portions of the manuscript and the looping that occurs in the published text reveal Gardner's exhaustive method of composition in which ideas and techniques are tested as he creates a work of fiction. Yet the complexity of the novel's structure, suggested by Gardner's notes, and the many variants of text Gardner struggled to get right also reveal that for Gardner the novel was as ambitious an undertaking as *The Sunlight Dialogues* and *Mickelsson's Ghosts*. More important to this study, the published parts of *Shadows* display possibilities for an intense working-out of the process—the testing of values—that is the heart of Gardner's fiction. Within the conventions of the murder mystery genre, Gardner wanted to explore again ways of explaining who we are and what we can know about ourselves and the world in which we live.[3]

The novel opens with a portrait of Gerald B. Craine, another of Gardner's aging and debilitated protagonists. Like Peter Mickelsson, Craine appears to be on the verge of a mental breakdown (in Fragment Seven of the published text Craine actually appears as a patient in a mental institution) and is filled with the guilt, paranoia, and dread shared by Gardner's older protagonists. More specifically, Craine is a washed-up and alcoholic private detective, once famous for his work

---

3. Suplee, "John Gardner, Flat Out," Washington *Post* (July 25, 1982), Sec. H, p. 9; Introduction to Gardner, *Stillness and Shadows*, xiv-xviii.

in Chicago but now semiretired in the small town of Carbondale, Illinois. The suspense of the opening chapters of Book I derives from Craine's feeling that he is being watched and from the warning given him by the mad prophet and magician Two-heads Carnac: " 'Strange forces is converging' " (186). As the narrative progresses, Gardner explores Craine's "wreckage" and offers alternatives to Craine's suspicion that existentialism may be the only way to cope with a meaningless universe. Another of Gardner's major interests in the novel is the concept of time, and by placing Craine in an alcoholic stupor throughout Book I, Gardner is able to suggest how altered states of consciousness may affect our perceptions of past, present, and future. Book I ends after someone assaults Carnac and murders April Vaught, a friend of Craine's neighbor, the poet Ira Katz. Craine begins to sober up when he is drawn into the murder investigation, for April appears to have been the sixth victim of a serial killer on the loose in Carbondale.

Instead of continuing this narrative line, Book II opens with an alternate introduction of Gerald Craine. This "looping" of the text may simply be, as Delbanco suggests, a variant of the opening chapter of Book I, for the first chapter of Book II repeats much of the information about Craine but substitutes interesting character sketches of Craine's associates for the slow-moving dialogues on reality and illusion, time and memory, and parapsychology that open Book I. Book II, in my opinion, also creates more suspense through the challenge and capture of Elaine Glass and generates interest through the establishment of a relationship between Elaine and Craine. Since most of Gardner's novels begin with some kind of dramatic action—Mickelsson bludgeons a dog to death, Taggert Hodge challenges Fred Clumly, Grendel is caught in a tree and nearly killed, Agathon and Peeker are arrested—Gardner may have decided that the dialogues between Craine and Dr. Tummelty and Inspector McClaren in Book I were too slow for the opening of a novel, especially one such as *Shadows* which relies upon the conventions of the murder mystery to generate suspense. The quicker pace of Book II and Delbanco's note that the opening lines of Book II are the opening lines of the novel in several of the manuscript variants suggest that Gardner may have decided to begin *Shadows* with Book II.

Another possibility, and a more intriguing one, is that both Book I and Book II would have remained intact in the novel. If we remember that Gardner's notes on the novel reveal his desire to have the narrative resemble "a huge computer product, routines and subroutines (given sub-themes recurrently plugged in to a larger program)," the digressions, slips in time, and looping in the manuscript and in the published text may reflect this computer-program model (xvi). Further evidence for such a structural experiment is supported, I think, by Fragment Two, in which computer scientist Murray Weintraub explains to Craine the obsession of computer hackers with the alternate realities they create through their programs, an obsession resembling that of fiction writers with the worlds they create in their stories and novels. As Gardner's notes reveal, he wishes to find out whether computer programmers are in any sense artists — "is it 'power' they love, or beauty?" (xvi). Although one might easily read all sorts of intentions into an incomplete manuscript, Gardner's experimentation with structure in previous novels, most notably in *Grendel, October Light*, and *Freddy's Book*, and his concern with various perceptions of reality in *Shadows* support my feeling that Gardner may have been more ambitious with *Shadows* than with any previous novel.

Whether we take Book I or Book II or both as the opening of *Shadows*, Gerald Craine's close resemblance to Fred Clumly and Peter Mickelsson is another bit of evidence that Gardner intended this novel to rival his major efforts of the 1960s and 1970s. Like Clumly and Mickelsson, Craine has become an eccentric and a figure of ridicule in the small town in which he lives. His career as a detective often overlaps Clumly's work in law enforcement, and he shares Mickelsson's keen interest in metaphysics. Craine's similarity to Mickelsson extends even to the questionable nature of the "second sight" both have inherited — just as Mickelsson's flashes and visions may be genuine or the result of poisoned water, Craine's may be genuine or the result of alcohol. Craine also has been successful at his profession, as have Clumly and Mickelsson: "They'd called Craine an artist, in his Chicago days, and they were right" (288). But like the police chief and the philosopher, Craine, and his "art," has lost touch with reality and with the community.

Typical of Gardner's protagonists, Craine is lost in despair at the beginning of the novel. His angst appears at first to be the result of a metaphysical disturbance, but he is also struggling with the very real presence of death. He has been operated on for a malignant cancer of the colon and is living with the threat of the disease's return. Although he insists he is not afraid of death, Craine, like James Chandler, is horrified that he may die without having any idea of *why* he has lived (333). Craine's insistence on solving this "mystery" leads him to much philosophical inquiry and reading, and like Gardner's other moral artists, he loves nothing more than to test his theories on people, especially those who are smug in their convictions or whose lives and ideas seem removed from his own.

Like James Chandler and Peter Mickelsson, however, Craine is a victim of his own intellectual search for truth. His belief, for instance, that a detective must embrace an existential view of life to be successful in his profession is an attempt to discover a system of behavior, a philosophy, to guide him through life. Craine wants to be " 'the man who solves the mystery . . . the solitary hunter, cold-blooded as the moon,' " like his heroes Sherlock Holmes and Hercule Poirot, men "from outside Time" (260). But he forgets that his heroes also had "loves" (Holmes for the violin and Poirot for detective fiction) and companions (Dr. Watson and Captain Hastings) to satisfy their emotional needs. As Gardner points out in his academic novels, *The Resurrection* and *Mickelsson's Ghosts*, a life devoted only to intellect is as limiting as one devoted only to feeling, and any attempt to discover a "system" of behavior is bound to fail. Craine's argument in support of existentialism is easily debunked by the poet Ira Katz: " 'I'll tell you the problem with existentialists. . . . They begin with the assumption that we're free — 'existence precedes essence' and all that. The trouble is, it's not true.' " " 'We obey the age-old law of mammals, the law that precedes our particular existence,' " Katz argues. " 'It seems to me that our proper business should be to try to figure out what the secret laws are for sentient mammals — what hurts us and what doesn't, physically, psychologically, spiritually. . . . We should work at discovering what values are built into us. Learn to survive — learn what makes us *fit*. The existentialists point us in the opposite direction, that's what's wrong with them. They encourage us to think we can make up values.' " Speaking even more directly for Gardner, Katz concludes his rebuttal by saying, " 'We have only two ways of finding out what's true, what will work. By history's blind groping, one damn thing after another, as they say . . . or by rigorous imagination, which in the end means by poems and novels' " (261–63).

Although Katz appears to have the moral artist's view of life, he is more likely the doomed artist of *Shadows*. As Gardner notes, Katz's collection of clocks and his "interest in linguistic reality" imply belief in a mechanistic universe that can be played off against his role as a poet (xvi). We also learn from Craine's later conversation with English Department chairman Wendell Davies that Katz's life is even more of a shambles than Craine's—his mother died a horrific death and blamed Katz for it with her dying words, he has for some reason walked out on his wife and two children, and his career as a teacher is in jeopardy because he refuses to publish for tenure. To make matters worse, Katz has been having an affair with the murdered woman April Vaught, and he has become involved in an impossibly ambitious project with members of the computer center to produce "a picture of the whole American reality." Like Craine, he wants to be the man who solves the mystery of existence, but his methods are as fruitless as Craine's because as artists both men have embraced their art to the exclusion of all else. Craine searches for some philosophical or scientific system that will allow him to solve the riddle of life, just as he uses various rational methods to solve crimes; and Katz has fooled "himself by claiming he was capturing life, that is, emotion in its flow, translating time into eternity" (409), when in fact his search for "connections" is futile because, like Craine, he has isolated himself from his family and the community, and he refuses to cooperate or compromise. An additional irony is that, at the same time Craine wants to be cold and objective, he is reading books on Hinduism and clairvoyance, and has more than a little interest in Katz's poetry.

Although he doubts the power of poetry, especially Katz's poetry, as a means of getting at truth (Katz's line, "Autumn, clear as the eyes of chickens," seems silly in its lack of connection with what Craine knows of the world), Craine senses some truth in Katz's life and words. As in all of Gardner's novels, the minor or doomed artist offers insight for the protagonist, and Katz's short discourse on "shadows" seems in a way the heart of the novel and provides at least one explanation of the dread Craine feels. Katz's theory also accounts for the human struggle to carry on even in the face of overwhelming evidence that existence has no purpose or meaning:

> "I have a theory," [Katz] said. "We have an idea of ourselves, when we're kids: noble-hearted, honorable, unselfish. It's a beautiful image, and in fact it's true—it's the truth about us—but we betray it, or the nature of the world betrays it. We betray it again and again, one way or another. We can't do what's decent. Our commitments prevent it, or it's beyond our means. . . . So we lose touch with ourselves, turn our backs on the image, believe ourselves to be the ugly thing we've by now half-proved we are. The image is still there, the shadow we cast into the future when we were young. It's still there haunting us, beckoning us toward it; only now there's that second shadow, the shadow, behind us, of all those acts unworthy of us." (268–69)

The shadow Craine has cast behind is apparently so "ugly" that he refuses to face it. In all of Gardner's novels, the protagonist comes to feel a nearly immobilizing guilt, either over responsibility for the death of another person or over betrayal of his family. Yet in the text we have of *Shadows*, Craine claims he has no memory of his personal past and does not appear to have a wife and children of his own. This is quite a divergence for a protagonist of Gardner's, since all of his artist figures share a deep attachment to the past (usually associated with the natural world) and often try to escape the modern world through memory or through some other means of recapturing the security and idyll of their youths. Craine's denial of the past, especially of his personal past, appears to Katz to be the source of Craine's problem. Craine is like the girl who witnessed a murder and never reported it, only to be haunted by the event—"snagged on . . . that unfulfilled moment," as Katz puts it. Whether Katz is correct or not, we never find out in the published text of *Shadows*, but Katz's guess that Craine's decline has been brought on by his denial of some unfulfilled moment in his past seems reasonable considering the effect of the past on protagonists in Gardner's other novels.

Craine chooses to "forget" the past, but his unconscious (where there is no distinction between past and present) provides additional evidence to support Katz's theory. Craine's inebriated state allows certain memories to rise from the depths, and, as we might expect, they are not pleasant. He associates his parents with death, his Aunt Harriet with repressed sexuality, and his grandfather with Bible-thumping religion. Consequently, he is filled with guilt and remorse when he considers either his family or questions concerning death, sex, or religion. He drinks to escape such feelings, thus creating a vicious circle of despair.

Whatever Craine is covering up in his past, he has little chance of dealing with it until he encounters the oddly attractive Elaine Glass. Although her character is not completely developed in what we have of *Shadows*, Elaine is clearly intended as the saintly intercessor of the novel. Hannah Johnson, Craine's black secretary, acts as a kind of motherly overseer to him, but not until Craine decides to protect Elaine Glass from the murderer who is stalking her does he feel that a woman has "switched on his denial-of-death machine . . . snapped Craine out of whatever he'd been in, headlong dive toward oblivion, withdrawal toward divinity and death" (326). Craine gradually begins to see in Elaine (and in Ira Katz) the same kind of withdrawal from life he has undergone. In fact, his ability to imagine what life must be like for Elaine and for Katz, as Henry Soames does for the doomed Simon Bale, is one of the great gifts of Gardner's moral artist: " 'It must be a terrible thing,' Craine tells Elaine, 'to live your whole life in a state of wild panic. . . . Afraid of tornadoes a month after the season for 'em, afraid of restaurants, afraid of phantoms wearing blue and white clothes. . . . Afraid of detectives, afraid of men' " (330). Craine pities her, as he pities himself, yet at the same time her touch and her presence move him: "for an instant, it seemed, he'd been in love with her" (334). Just as Peter Mickelsson denies his love for Jessica Stark, believing himself unworthy of her and at the same time scoffing at the power of love to alter life, Craine refuses to accept his feelings for Elaine. To avoid them, he denigrates himself and her: "He was nobody's friend, if he told himself the truth. Her damned Jewish neuroses, her self-absorbed daddy, her stifling mother, her sex-death fantasy of a blue-and-white pursuer—what were they to him? . . . Once the case was finished, he'd forget her in a week, or anyway forget how he'd felt for a minute a few minutes ago" (333). Craine's recognition of his problem is ironic, for when Elaine turns his question on him— " 'What is it *you're* afraid of?' "—Craine suggests it simply may be that he has "gotten separated from himself . . . gotten split off from his feelings" (332, 334). How Elaine helps in bringing about Craine's final reintegration we cannot know, but from the text Gardner has provided, we know she begins to move him from his tormented, drunken life back into contact with the world.

Although Craine has fled the city for the small town, he does not seem to have gained much comfort or security from "semiretirement" in Carbondale. The "dale of carbon" does not offer the natural beauty of Susquehanna in *Mickelsson's Ghosts* or of the Catskills in *Nickel Mountain*. Neither is Carbondale undergoing the kind of urbanization Gardner attributes to Batavia in *The Resurrection* and *The Sunlight Dialogues*. The town is depressing and in a state of decay: "finely sifted dust on car and truck fenders, the humps and jagged cracks in the sidewalk—grass pushing up through them, insects thriving on them, ants and wood ticks, ladybugs, mosquitoes . . . a universe stuffed like an old spinster's hope chest with junk" (199–200). What remains of the untamed forces of nature exists only in the destructive power of midwestern tornados, but they further contribute to the dread of the place and are predictably confined to certain months of the year. In none of Gardner's novels has a small town fallen so far from the Edenic ideal as Carbondale has in *Shadows*. The dreary gloom of Gerald Craine is "the normal gloom of Little Egypt," of southern Illinois and its natives. As in *The Sunlight Dialogues*, where Clumly's Edenic world is confined to the Batavia cemetery and to the ruin of the Hodge estate, in *Shadows* the natural world has been polluted and pillaged and forced into the remaining square blocks of the immaculately manicured university campus, which is the only place unaffected, or so Craine thinks, by time.

Even the peaceful campus has been invaded by "the real world" in the form of six murders that involve some teachers and students, and its ivy-towered beauty is undercut by the "cancerous" growth of the computer center to which Gardner lends an intentional ominousness in his description in Fragment Two. Just as the beauty of the natural world contains the ruthless and random process of evolution, so the "truth and beauty" of the university contains the random and uncontrollable proliferation of computers. As Gardner's notes for the novel indicate, he wanted to explore the lack of control we eventually may have over computers and to examine what people in a society run by computers may have to fear. Craine's cancer, Gardner believed, is somewhat analogous to the computer's enormously complex, team-derived programs. Whereas Craine is at the mercy of the cancer "programmed" into his cells over generations, a programmer is at the mercy of a computer whose program has been randomly developed over decades by various individuals with various aims. The beauty of the machine, whether we think of it as the natural world, the human body, or a complex computer, is always complemented by a darker side. Gardner never attempts to destroy the illusion of such beauty, but he does wish to warn us that we must eventually deal with this unknowable other.

In *Shadows*, the view of the world is perhaps bleaker than in any previous novel, but Gardner allows Craine to hold onto the "shadow cast into the future." In Fragment Five, as he stands in a classroom building and gazes out a window upon the campus, Craine sees the world transformed into "some noble old painting from the eighteenth century." Craine knows that the beauty of the trees, the grass, the slant of light are real, but he also knows that his vision is enhanced by his feelings for Elaine Glass, who is a student at the university, and by his own imagination, where the Edenic ideal exists undiminished by the shadow he has cast behind him:

> All this while Craine stood motionless, staring out the window like a man in a trance, watching the sky change, dark, silvered cloud patches moving northward through the yellow, reflected in the windows of the buildings across from him, the leaves of the trees moving . . . and he was thinking . . . *Strange, how beautiful it is, how peaceful!* It was true, no mere illusion, he understood, not quite in words. It was not just that it seemed like some noble old painting, though it did, certainly; on the campus time had in some quite real sense stopped. Everyone noticed it, if only in jest. People distinguished between the campus and "the real world." It was the last playground; that might be it, perhaps. The last slow, easy breath of childhood. (410–11)

For the observer, Craine thinks, campus is a place where "*time does not exist*" (411). The absence or unimportance of time in the Edenic world is connected somehow in Craine's mind with the absence or unimportance of time in the Freudian unconscious, particle physics, and psychic experience — three areas of interest to Craine in his search for answers. For Gardner, these three means of explaining the world roughly parallel the three traditional branches of metaphysics — psychology, cosmology, and ontology, which may in turn bear some relationship to Craine's unpleasant memories of sex, death, and religion. What Gardner may have made of this collection of "trinities" is unclear, but Craine gains stability as he incorporates some of the "modern" metaphysical explanations of human behavior into his own system of thought, and certainly his rediscovery of the Edenic campus and the arousal of long-forgotten feelings brought on by his relationship with Elaine Glass counter his gloomy existence.

Although he continues to think of himself as only an observer, divorced from the academic pretense of university people and from the uncivilized "crocodiles" of the Bible Belt, Craine has been accepted by the people of Carbondale and has become a member of the community despite his eccentric behavior: "Carnac was Carbondale's one authentic lunatic, if you didn't count Craine" (184). When memories of his cancer operation slip up on him, Craine is surprised to recall how many people care for him: "Friends — acquaintances — came by, sent cards, wakened him with phone calls, sent flowers. It was astonishing that he, testy, cold-blooded old bastard that he was, should be so rich in friends or anyway acquaintances." And "snarl as he might, it was [his] nature to assume that even the most despicable of mortals had something to be said for him. . . . He defended the indefensible, blanched at nothing, mothered the monstrous" (235). "If anyone had pushed him, he'd have admitted more: that he was glad to see them. Sometimes when one of them came grinning through the door, Craine's eyes, to his shame and indignation, would well up with tears. He was tempted to say to himself, 'Life means more than you thought, you old fart. Look how many people, as the saying goes, "care" ' " (236). Compassion allows Craine a certain freedom as well, and as he takes up the practice of visiting his neighbors in the hospital ward, "he walked in a bubble of time exactly like childhood time," so that the patients and their families form a community of sorts.

Craine also gains some sense of community from his associates in the agency. Each of them unconsciously plays the role of a family member: Tom Meakins, the worried yet ineffectual father; Hannah Johnson, the overly protective mother; Emmit Royce, the wild, uncontrollable teenager; and Craine, at once the eccentric son and debilitated patriarch. Since Craine hand-picked his associates, we can assume he has created this surrogate family to replace the one he has "forgotten." From these communities, tucked one within the other in Craine's mind, we understand the value of human contact, but Craine continues to believe life is "by no means a matter for joyful celebration" (240). Although Gardner probably intended "a communion of souls" for *Shadows*, we do not have a gathering, as we do in previous novels, where the protagonist has a moment of grace, a chance to break through the impasse he faces. Yet from the disparate characters Craine encounters and from the precedent-setting importance of community values in Gardner's previous novels, I believe the narrative is moving toward the kind of detective novel denouement that involves a gathering of all those caught up in the mystery of the murder and in the mystery of life. We can only assume that if Gardner had followed the convention of murder mysteries, the killer—the ominous stranger of *Shadows*—would be unveiled at this gathering and Craine would already have gained from him or her the information necessary to aid him in his journey toward reintegration. But this is only speculation.

Craine, as an artist, is perhaps in worse shape than any of Gardner's other protagonists, yet the published text of *Shadows* suggests that Craine, unlike the failed artists Grendel, Taggert Hodge, and Agathon, will be a survivor. Despite the cancer, the drinking, the mental illness, the existential dread, Craine has a myriad of ideas and thoughts to explore. And despite his tendency to irritate and attack others, Craine is receptive, open, and cautious—traits that once made him a good detective and that will now aid him in discovering the truth about his life. As Craine solves the murder mystery, he presumably will solve many of his own problems and again become a part of the world from which he has retreated, just as in writing fiction, the artist withdraws into his imagination and explores his own feelings in order to create a work of art that makes contact with his readers. If Gardner had lived to "fix" *Shadows*, I have no doubt that from Craine's reintegration we would have once again discovered "the connectedness of all things" that arises from making life art.

6
Conclusion
A Brief Evaluation
of the Novels

Although I would prefer not to assess the relative importance of each of Gardner's novels in relation to the others, such an assessment is usually expected of any serious study of a writer's works and, in this instance, is probably dictated also by my approach to the novels. As I have mentioned, in trying to draw attention to neglected works—*The Resurrection, The Wreckage of Agathon, Nickel Mountain*—and to the novels dismissed by reviewers—*Mickelsson's Ghosts, Freddy's Book*—I have intentionally downplayed the significance of Gardner's most acclaimed and perhaps best works—*The Sunlight Dialogues, October Light, Grendel.*

It would be folly to differ with the general consensus concerning the ultimate importance of *The Sunlight Dialogues.* Gardner's firm allegiance to the strategies and theories of the nineteenth-century novel and novelist allows him to handle the material of his only architectonic novel with the skill of a Melville or a Tolstoy or a Henry James. The intricacies of the book and Gardner's careful attention to details —from the symbolic names of characters to the realistic depiction of a small town being dragged into the twentieth century—fuse the stories of one man's obsession and revenge and another's fears and doubts into Gardner's nearly perfect work of "moral fiction."

I will differ, however, in assessing the novel of greatest significance next to *The Sunlight Dialogues,* for I favor the much-maligned *Mickelsson's Ghosts* over such popular choices as *Grendel* and *October*

Light. Not only is *Mickelsson's Ghosts* another of the "loose baggy monsters" Gardner admired, but it is also a *tour de force* in the modern psychological novel. As Larry Woiwode has written, "it's a novel that no writer but Gardner could have imagined, in all its wit and intellectual acumen, much less produced, and this is surely the reason it has met with the resistance it has; no reader or reviewer has been able to fit his mind around the originality of its contours."[1]

Gardner's mastery of the novel as a genre is also apparent in *October Light*. Although some reviewers and critics have condemned his use of the inner novel as an irritating interruption of James Page's story, I think the success of the novel depends on *The Smugglers of Lost Souls' Rock*. This parody of the kind of contemporary fiction, with its emphasis on sex and violence, that Gardner thought irresponsible keeps the narrative of Sally and James Page from lapsing into the sentimentality and melodrama inherent in the traditional novel of social observation that Gardner otherwise admired. A balance is achieved through the stand-off of narratives.

Not coincidentally, *The Sunlight Dialogues, Mickelsson's Ghosts*, and *October Light* are Gardner's longest works as well as his best novels. The reintegrations of the protagonists are so well prepared for and the "process" of moral fiction is so fully developed that the final scenes of these novels are striking in their revelations yet acceptable within the contexts of what has happened to Fred Clumly, Peter Mickelsson, and James Page. Gardner's process works better in these books simply because the characters are developed beyond the "types" that we see in some of his stories and because the narratives are more complex than the allegories of *Grendel* and *Freddy's Book*.

Only after these three novels would I rank *Grendel*, Gardner's most popular work. The book's success is due to Gardner's sheer cleverness in retelling *Beowulf* and his use of fashionable metafictional techniques. These characteristics, however, will eventually result in a lessening of interest in the novel, although I am sure it will survive, along with *The Life and Times of Chaucer*, as a source of envy, amusement, and controversy among medieval scholars. The novel's strength, beneath the complexities of organization and style that have been so thoroughly explicated, is the simplicity of its message. Grendel is the monster in each of us, but Gardner's point is that we can feel compas-

---

1. Larry Woiwode, "*Mickelsson's Ghosts*: Gardner's Memorial in Real Time," *MSS*, IV (Fall, 1984), 317.

sion for even the most horrible of those among us, as we do for Grendel. Compassion breeds hope, and Grendel has neither. He is to be pitied but never admired for his nihilistic view of the universe.

Among Gardner's lesser works, *The Resurrection, The Wreckage of Agathon*, and *Freddy's Book* are of equal significance. As I have suggested, parts of these novels reveal Gardner at his best as a storyteller and also initiate some of the more interesting techniques and ideas he developed in his longer works that followed or, in the case of *Freddy's Book*, may have developed later had he lived. In a sense, *The Resurrection, The Wreckage of Agathon*, and *Freddy's Book* are experimental works. In *The Resurrection*, Gardner breaks from the limited point of view of *Nickel Mountain* and discovers a "true 19th-century omniscient voice." *The Wreckage of Agathon* is the first of Gardner's "fabulistic" novels and prepares the way for *Grendel* and for *The Sunlight Dialogues* in its use of ancient history and in its development of an artist/protagonist who is doomed to failure. And *Freddy's Book*, in its organization and style, raises all sorts of speculation and debate over what form Gardner might have used in "historical" novels that would have followed.

Although I have a special fondness for *Nickel Mountain*, its origin as a collection of short stories and Gardner's decision to fuse them into a novel account for the discontinuity most readers sense upon completing the book.[2] *Nickel Mountain* contains some powerful depictions of human loneliness and interaction, but the characters are, for the most part, types, and Henry Soames's transformation at the end of the novel is imbued with a mysticism Gardner avoids in the seven novels that follow this work of his apprenticeship.

John Gardner's novels, while embodying ideas that may be disagreeable to contemporary writers and literary critics, are of major importance to American fiction. His innovative techniques alone are worthy of lengthy study, and when we consider that such experimentation in Gardner's hands also seeks what Faulkner called "eternal verities"—truths pursued by literary genius through the ages—we begin to see more clearly the valuable role Gardner plays in the development of our literature and what contribution he makes to the novel in particular.

2. Howell, "The Wound and the Albatross," 8–9.

Bibliography

Primary Sources

Gardner, John. *The Art of Fiction*. New York, 1984.

_____. *The Art of Living and Other Stories*. New York, 1981.

_____. *Freddy's Book*. New York, 1980.

_____. *Grendel*. New York, 1971.

_____. *In the Suicide Mountains*. New York, 1977.

_____. *The King's Indian: Stories and Tales*. New York, 1974.

_____. *The Life and Times of Chaucer*. New York, 1977.

_____. *Mickelsson's Ghosts*. New York, 1982.

_____. *Nickel Mountain*. New York, 1973.

_____. *October Light*. New York, 1976.

_____. *On Becoming a Novelist*. New York, 1983.

_____. *On Moral Fiction*. New York, 1978.

_____. *The Resurrection*. Rev. ed. New York, 1974.

_____. *Stillness and Shadows*. Edited by Nicholas Delbanco. New York, 1986.

_____. *The Sunlight Dialogues*. New York, 1972.

_____. *The Wreckage of Agathon*. New York, 1970.

Secondary Sources

A. Books

Bellamy, Joe David. *The New Fiction: Interviews with Innovative American Writers*. Urbana, Ill., 1974.

_____, ed. *Moral Fiction: An Anthology*. Canton, N.Y., 1980.

Cowart, David. *Arches and Light: The Fiction of John Gardner*. Carbondale, Ill., 1983.

Encyclopedia of Philosophy. Edited by Paul Williams. Volumes I and II. New York, 1967.

Henderson, Jeff, ed. *Thor's Hammer: Essays on John Gardner*. Conway, Ark., 1985.

Howell, John. *John Gardner: A Bibliographical Profile*. Carbondale, Ill., 1980.

Kubler-Ross, Elisabeth. *On Death and Dying*. New York, 1969.

Mendez-Egle, Beatrice, ed. *John Gardner: True Art, Moral Art*. Living Author Series No. 5. Edinburg, Tex., 1983.

Morace, Robert A. *John Gardner: An Annotated Secondary Bibliography*. New York, 1984.

_____, and Kathryn VanSpanckeren, eds. *John Gardner: Critical Perspectives*. Carbondale, Ill., 1982.

Morris, Gregory L. *A World of Order and Light: The Fiction of John Gardner*. Athens, Ga., 1984.

Reiman, Donald H., and Sharon B. Powers, eds. *Shelley's Poetry and Prose*. New York, 1977.

Squires, Michael. *The Pastoral Novel: Studies in George Eliot, Thomas Hardy, and D. H. Lawrence*. Charlottesville, Va., 1974.

Stevens, Wallace. *Collected Poems of Wallace Stevens*. New York, 1982.

B. Articles, Essays, and Interviews

Christian, Ed. "An Interview with John Gardner." *Prairie Schooner*, LIV (Winter, 1980–81), 70–93.

Coale, Samuel. " 'Into the Farther Darkness': The Manichean Pastoralism of John Gardner." In *John Gardner: Critical Perspectives*, edited by Robert A. Morace and Kathryn VanSpanckeren. Carbondale, Ill., 1982.

Ferguson, Paul F., *et al.* "John Gardner: The Art of Fiction LXXIII." *Paris Review,* XXI (Spring, 1979), 36–74.

Harvey, Marshall L. "Where Philosophy and Fiction Meet: An Interview with John Gardner." *Chicago Review*, XXIX (Spring, 1978), 73–87.

Henderson, Jeff. "The Avenues of Mundane Salvation: Time and Change in the Fiction of John Gardner." *American Literature*, LV (1983), 611–33.

_____. "John Gardner's Layered Fiction: The Supernatural and the Paranatural." In *Thor's Hammer: Essays on John Gardner*, edited by Jeff Henderson. Conway, Ark., 1985.

Howell, John. "The Wound and the Albatross: John Gardner's Apprenticeship." In *Thor's Hammer: Essays on John Gardner*, edited by Jeff Henderson. Conway, Ark., 1985.

Johnson, Charles. "A Phenomenology of *On Moral Fiction*." In *Thor's Hammer: Essays on John Gardner*, edited by Jeff Henderson. Conway, Ark., 1985.

Larson, Elizabeth. "The Creative Act: An Analysis of Systems in *Grendel*." In *John Gardner: True Art, Moral Art*, edited by Beatrice Mendez-Egle. Living Author Series No. 5. Edinburg, Tex., 1983.

Minugh, David. "John Gardner Constructs *Grendel's* Universe." In *Studies in English Philology, Linguistics, and Literature: Presented to Alarik Rynell (March 7, 1978)*, edited by Mats Ryden and Lennart A. Bjork. Stockholm Studies in English, XLVI. Stockholm, 1978.

Morace, Robert A. "*Freddy's Book*, Moral Fiction, and Writing as a Mode of Thought." *Modern Fiction Studies*, XXIX (Summer, 1983), 201-12.

Singular, Stephen. "The Sound and Fury over Fiction." *New York Times Magazine* (July 8, 1979), 12-15, 34-36, 38-39.

Strehle, Susan. "John Gardner's Novels: Affirmation and the Alien." *Critique*, XVIII (1976), 86-96.

Stromme, Craig J. "The Twelve Chapters of *Grendel*." *Critique*, XX (1978), 83-92.

Suplee, Curt. "John Gardner, Flat Out." Washington *Post*, July 25, 1982, Sec. H., pp. 1, 8-9.

Winther, Per. "An Interview with John Gardner." *English Studies*, LXII (December, 1981), 509-24.

Woiwode, Larry. "*Mickelsson's Ghosts*: Gardner's Memorial in Real Time." *MSS*, IV (Fall, 1984), 315-30.

Index